The Truth About Book Reviews

★★★★★

An Insider's Guide to Getting and Using
Reviews to **Grow Your Readership**

JOE WALTERS

Publisher: IBR Books

First Edition: July 2025

Cover Design: Jaylynn Korrell

ISBN (ebook): 979-8-9986577-1-9

ISBN (Paperback): 979-8-9986577-0-2

For permissions & publicity, contact jwalters@independentbookreview.com.

CONTENTS

INTRODUCTION

G etting a book review is like eavesdropping on a dream conversation. Someone is talking about your book in the wild. What
they're saying might mean the world to you, but that's not why they're
talking. This is not to boost your ego like a friend or help you improve
like an editor. They're reviewing your book to tell another reader, someone like them, whether their precious, limited reading hours should be
spent on you.

You won't get that kind of honesty or insight anywhere else.

Even when the reviewer is wrong, they are still a reflection of your
audience: the people who buy your book (sometimes by mistake), who
read your newsletters, who decide to stay with you or leave. They are the
ones you are writing to—the ones who matter most.

I'm not saying you have to agree with everything your critics say about
you, but I am saying you should be listening to how they are saying it.
Are a lot of people recommending your book with five stars and heart
eyes, or are most of them leading with criticism and a shoulder shrug?
Are people misunderstanding what you were trying to do? Or worse, are
they choosing not to review you at all?

Every author, expert, blogger, and vlogger has told you: you need to
get book reviews if you want to sell books. They're essential validation.
They influence everyday readers to buy or pass, and they do the same

with bookstore owners and librarians. I mean—even the number of book reviews matters in marketing.

But they're more than just this powerful marketing tool. They're your way in. The truth about book reviews is this:

> ## Book reviews are the best way to tell if you are doing this whole thing right.

The writing, the editing, the revising, the designing, the marketing. All of it.

If you can get book reviews, you can get book sales. Not in the sense that sales will come flooding in once you hit a certain number of them, but rather, if you can convince enough strangers to leave reviews for you, you have created a strong enough product to sell—from cover to description to blurbs to content and beyond. Book reviews are the ultimate publishing litmus test.

In editing, you learn how to tell your best story, but you don't learn the real reason that people aren't buying it is the cover. Even spying on your KDP dashboard won't tell you how you've done with the book's content. You can sell an imperfect book (for a while). But if you aren't getting reviews after those sales, or if multiple people are telling you the same thing is wrong, you'll gain insight that can change your career.

Reviews don't just come to you though. Not yet anyway.

You need to find reviewers first, and then you need to convince them to review it. But how do you do that?

There's no magic button to press, but there are more strategies you can use to get them than you have the time for. The real goal is to get reviews efficiently—to get it right the first time. That's where I come in.

I've been getting book reviews for indie authors for almost a decade now. From Marketing & Publicity Director at one publishing house to Book Review and Metadata Specialist at another, I spent years testing out strategies to see what worked in increasing book sales.

Like all actively marketing indie authors, I had a parade of things I could do for my publishers to sell books: write descriptions and bios, do keyword research, create catalogs and press releases, send newsletters, post on social media, design graphics, build review teams; you name it, I did it. I focused on what the publishers needed most and used my paid time in a way that could make them and their authors money.

But I had hundreds of books to market and years to figure it out. I can't give you the freedom to market your book full-time or give you hundreds of books to experiment and learn from, but I can give you this: a compendium of what I've learned; all my minutes, my failures, and my triumphs in the category I have the most experience in—book reviews.

Because not only have I pitched hundreds of books for review over my small press career—got yeses and nos and crickets chirping—but I've seen things from the other side of the pitch too.

When I found out just how many books there were and how few platforms there were to cover them, I made one—for indies only.

I launched Independent Book Review (IBR) in 2018. My plan was to be reader-focused and writer-supportive. We'd recommend cool, little-known books to readers while making authors' and presses' jobs easier.

And now, seven years later, we've reviewed over 2,000 indie books, from traditional reviews to book lists, and I spend my work day reading about books and choosing which ones to feature on my website. I make decisions based on what has driven affiliate income book sales and site traffic in the past and which ones look too good to pass up on.

In this book, you get all of it. Both sides: marketer and reviewer. What you need to do before publishing, what to do during and after launch—you're going to walk out of here with the knowledge and ability to get more book reviews and to use them to elevate your author career.

You've got work to do. Let's get to it.

PART 1: WHAT YOU NEED TO KNOW ABOUT BOOK REVIEWS

1

THE THREE TYPES OF BOOK REVIEWS

B efore you go on your epic review-chasing journey, you're going to want to know what you're looking for.

You probably already know this definition:

> Book reviews are assessments of an author's work written for readers and book buyers to help them decide whether they should buy a copy for themselves or their stores.

But there are three different kinds.

Since you are steering the ship of this book business, you'll want to separate your work time into targeting each type of book review. I wouldn't call them different departments at your publishing company, but they do have different chairs.

This chapter outlines the three types of book reviews in timeline order.

#1. Blurbs (or editorial reviews)

Blurbs (or editorial reviews) are short book reviews written by authors or experts in the book's field.

Authors or publishers get blurbs so they can use them in their marketing materials like book covers, press releases, websites, graphics, their Amazon page, book descriptions, and more. A praiseworthy blurb from the right individual or platform can turn a skeptic into a believer, a browser into a buyer.

You will want to start pursuing blurbs as soon as a suitable draft is available. This could mean a year in advance or three months if you don't have that kind of time.

While it's beneficial to get blurbs months before publication, you can kind of get them whenever you want. If you have a chance to get Stephen King to write something nice about your book after it is published, you should not say no thank you.

#2. Media and trade reviews

Media reviews are just what they sound like: reviews in the media.

Websites, magazines, newspapers, podcasts, YouTube, Instagram, TikTok, TV—if they're talking about your book without you there and it's not on a sales page or Goodreads, it's a media review.

It is beneficial to start pitching for media reviews a few months before publication, but you can keep pitching with some success for around a year after publication—maybe longer if your topic is timely or evergreen, like your picture book is still about Easter three years later. Social media reviews are evergreen too, so you can keep pitching for those for as long as your book is relevant.

Trade reviews are what industry people call book review-specific platforms. Trade reviews come from recognized book experts in the field, and these publications are written for other members in the book industry. Readers peruse these sites, but the platform's focus may be geared more toward trying to get book buyers at stores and libraries to notice, trust, and stock books.

Some trade publications require a long lead-up time, which means they require a pitch six months in advance of publication. So if you want trade reviews, you'll want to start this process around seven months before publication. This means research, perfecting the pitch and product, and maybe even printing physical advance review copies (ARCs) if the platform requires it.

If you don't qualify for this (like if your book isn't ready that far in advance), you're going to be fine. Your book won't die and you won't either. Indie authors hit a lot of roadblocks during this adventure; this book is about jumping over them and moving forward.

#3. Customer reviews (Amazon & Goodreads)

Last but not least is an understatement. Customer reviews might be the most important of the three types of book reviews.

Customer reviews are reviews from everyday people—bookish or not. If they read often and are part of the online book community, they may leave their reviews in places like Goodreads or StoryGraph, but most non-bookies leave their reviews on Amazon. In your own review targeting, I'd recommend pursuing Amazon as your primary customer review platform with Goodreads and StoryGraph as consolation prizes.

There's a longer list of customer review locations (like Apple and Barnes & Noble in Part 4 of this book).

You can't get reviews on Amazon until the book is available for purchase, but you can start pursuing them about two months in advance by researching, setting up launch teams, and scheduling launch-time advertising. You can get reviews on Goodreads before publication, but you'll need a few things (like a website and ISBN) to set up the book page first.

What customer reviews say doesn't matter as much as the number of reviews that you have. The difference between a book with 150 reviews versus a book with four is substantial. Some reviews arrive on Amazon without you doing anything—a true gift from the review gods—but most of them won't.

It's up to you.

THE 3 TYPES OF REVIEWS

BLURBS (OR EDITORIAL REVIEWS)

Short book reviews written by authors or experts in the book's field.

- **Often found** on book covers, graphics, press releases and opening pages.

MEDIA & TRADE REVIEWS

Book reviews published or spoken about on literary & media platforms —digital, print, or audio.

- **Examples:** *Independent Book Review, Publisher's Weekly, People*

CUSTOMER REVIEWS

Book reviews from everyday people— bookish or not.

- **Examples:** Amazon & Goodreads

2

THE ESSENTIALS

HOW TO INCREASE YOUR CHANCES OF BEING REVIEWED (PART 1)

There is no secret formula when it comes to pitching books for review. But some practices will give you a better chance than others.

This chapter is about getting your foundation strong and sturdy before you go pitching anyone. If you excel in these categories, your chances of getting reviewed are going to go up.

Since it's never only about the foundation, we'll talk in part two of this dual chapter about the intangibles that increase your chances even more. For now, let's follow the submission guidelines, design incredible covers, write strong book descriptions, and send that all-important pitch letter.

#1. Follow the submission guidelines.

Nothing is more important than this. You're going to be pitching a lot of people after reading this book. You could listen to every piece of advice in it and come out totally dejected and near review-less if you don't reach out to the right person or provide what they ask for. You won't get reviewed if your pitch isn't being seen, and they won't double-check if you didn't send something they need. They have a process. Work with it, not against it.

If the company or person you are pitching has a website, you will want to find their Submission Guidelines page. If it's not called that, look for "Review Policy" or "For Authors/Publishers." If you can't find any of these, check out their "Contact," "Team," or "About" pages; they will likely have a link or information regarding what authors/publishers should do to send their pitches. They usually require materials like the full book (physical or digital), cover, description, genre, release date, and ISBN. They will also give you a very specific email you're supposed to send the pitch to. If it tells you to do this, definitely send it there. Don't send it to a personal email just because you believe it will be seen there, unless you have a personal connection with that specific person.

Some media platforms, bloggers, or customer reviewers won't have a submission guidelines page at all. So you'll be tasked with sending your best pitch in your style, and that's it. My recommendation for this would be to include your cover and a short pitch letter—without the book.

#2. Design the best book cover.

Oh, man, the power of a great book cover! It's going to influence everything you do in marketing: from reviews to sales to events to shelving and beyond. Some reviewers and buyers will make decisions on whether to get a book on cover alone, even if many others read about the author and story.

The cover is essential for every pitch. Whether you attach it to the email or link to it in the pitch, your recipient is going to use it to decide whether or not to read your book. It's the first thing they see, so make it good.

I used to put the cover right in the body of the email, just above a shorter version of the description, but the more I shared that advice with my authors, the more I saw that not every emailer is set up well for that. If you put it in the wrong size in the body of your email or can't figure out how to align it correctly, it could negatively impact the professionalism of your pitch. (I still think it can work if you're good at it.)

Like agents, I receive a ton of book submissions at Independent Book Review. I don't have the time to read every second of every pitch, so I start with the subject line and book cover without even opening the email. If the cover doesn't look like it could entice a random stranger to buy it, I mark that email as read and move on. Don't be that book.

If you're designing your cover, you better be good at graphic design. And you better come up with at least three different concepts and countless drafts to get it right.

It's usually safest to focus on one or two primary elements so that there's not too much to look at. You'll also need to use the right font in the right, natural spot on the cover.

No matter how confident you are, get feedback on it from your beta readers and maybe a Facebook group you interact with and trust. Friends and family can give feedback, but just know they might not know your genre the way that you and other voracious readers and writers do. Matching genre is an incredibly important part of this, so make sure you peruse the Amazon bestseller pages of your genres. (You can find them by visiting the product details on your Amazon page.) Take a look at other covers in your niche so you can match but also stand out in your design. Readers and reviewers should know at first glance which genre it fits in.

If you're hiring a designer (or multiple), you're probably making the right decision. But it's not as simple as handing over money. You're going to need to tell your designer what you envision for your cover. They're not going to read your book to get it. They'll make the creative decisions necessary to make your vision work, so they might shoot an idea or two down, but they'll need your guidance up front. You'll most likely need a short description (100-150 words MAX), the genres, the potential colors, tones, and comp covers.

If you get a cover from your designer you don't like, you could either choose to give them another shot or move on without them. Covers are incredibly important, so if you feel like you're not happy with the work they did, it probably isn't going to help to pay them for another mockup. Count your losses and move on; definitely don't use a cover that you and your testers don't love.

#3. Choose a great title and subtitle.

For fiction, a good title can be almost as influential as a good cover. It can be long and poetic, short and sharp, mysterious and exciting. No matter what, it should fit your genre and avoid cliche as often as possible: Do you need the "The?" Should you talk of the "[Something] Within?" Every title needs something different. The most important thing to do is get feedback on it. Give people options, see which ones win, and base it off of whether the reader is given an excuse to read it.

Some fiction books can get away with smart subtitles, like *The Last Thing I'll Ever Write: Part One* by Adam Lauver, or by including a strong keyword or trope. Keywords are phrases that customers type into their Amazon search bar, like "small town mystery," while tropes are well-loved genre storylines, like amateur female sleuths in women's fiction. Author Sherilyn Decter does a good job with these (*Big Sky Murder: Which is safer? Being an outlaw or being an outcast? Sometimes a woman has to choose.*) as well as books from *Joffe Books*, a prolific British crime-mystery thriller publisher.

For nonfiction, subtitles are among your book's most important selling points. Not only can your book be found strictly through keywords in your subtitle, but it can communicate exactly what your reader will gain from reading the book. The more the reviewer knows going in about what the book will discuss, the more they'll be drawn to picking it up.

Some of the best nonfiction subtitles I've worked on:

- *W.G.: The Opium-addicted Pistol Toting Preacher Who Raised the First Federal African American Union Troops* by William & Donna Burtch

- *Help Yourself Every Day: Thirty Magical Meditations to Boost Your Emotional Well-Being* by Catherine Depino

- *Baseball's Greatest What-If: The Story & Tragedy of the Brooklyn Dodgers' Pistol Pete Reiser* by Dan Joseph

- *Something Like Treason: Disloyal American Soldiers & the Plot to Bring World War II Home* by William Sonn

---

#4. Write a stellar book description featuring your best content.

Strap in! This section is long and important. We'll be talking about how book descriptions affect book review pitches and how to write them for different categories: novels, nonfiction books, and collections.

When I assign books to my reviewers at IBR, I send them the book size, the genre, the cover, and the book description. That's it. They don't get your pitch, chock-full of blurbs and press material.

I already told you: reviewers are looking at the book cover first, testing out the feel of it and its conjunction with the title. Then they move on to the practical, whether they have the time and availability to read and review a book of this size at this timeline. Then comes the book description, where the final decision is made.

In your description, reviewers learn if the book has real momentum or if it fluffs up only one storyline. Readers can recognize whether your book meshes well with the genre they love and if it offers anything new or promising to it. It can even provide subtle content warnings to dissuade the wrong kind of reviewer from taking the book on in the first place. And you need it (or a version of it) with every pitch.

When pitching reviewers, you will either include your book's entire description (like the one for Amazon) or you can use a portion of it, perhaps even personalizing it for specific recipients. Saving their time is often a good move, but some reviewers (like me!) actually want the full description as part of their process. As always, **follow those submission guidelines**.

Writing and editing book descriptions was definitely among my favorite tasks at my other jobs. Not only did I get to write a little story in my work time, honing in on my skills with practice, but book descriptions work when you're away from the computer. After you write and perfect it, it's always on your product page, doing its job in converting browsers into buyers or prospective reviewer into a review. Here's how to do it right.

How to Write Novel & Memoir Descriptions

I'll always recommend opening a book description with a bold-ed hook.

For most authors, it's more likely that prospective readers find their descriptions on a device rather than on the back cover at a bookstore. And reading on a device is much different than in a book—show me the person who reads every word of every digital article nowadays and I'll show you my surprised face. So make scanning easy on them with paragraph breaks, keywords, and a dynamic first line.

Bold it too. Make sure those readers who don't prioritize descriptions read your best selling point right away. The hook should be punchy and short, usually less than fifteen words.

Here are a few things you could try as a hook:

- Highlight a much loved trope in a fresh way—i.e. "Friends to lovers," "Race against time," etc.

- Include your book's most popular or intriguing keyword—i.e. "Romantasy," "Locked room mystery," "Road trip," etc.

- Use quotes from your best blurb.

- Mention your best accolades, like "Named a Book of the Year by *Library Journal* and Independent Book Review."

- Mention a comparable title or two.

- Hint at an explosive inciting incident.

- Encompass your main theme(s).

- Ask the main question your book is asking.

- Portend how your book solves a common problem.

Examples of strong hooks:

- *"Dept. of Speculation* **meets** *Black Mirror* **in this lyrical, speculative debut about a queer mother raising her daughter in an unjust surveillance state."** - from *I Keep My Exoskeletons to Myself* by Marisa Crane

- **"Every school has a secret."** - *Faces In a Window* by Oliver C. Seneca

- **"When the popular crowd at Brentwood High votes me Most Likely To: Marry A Math Book, I'm ready to put my ruler into the eye of any egotistical jock who comes near me."** - *Teaching the Teacher's Pet* by Sarah Sutton

- **"Rule #1 of the Underground Railroad: If someone doesn't need to know something, don't tell them."** - *The Conductor* by Roger A. Smith

But the hook is only the first line!

You've got at least three, probably four, maybe seven more paragraph breaks to go. I like between 125-200 words for fiction book descriptions. You might think "the shorter, the better" since we want to make things easy and enticing for the reader, but too short of a description can fail to communicate what and whom the book is about. Try to hit that recommended word count and make sure the content is spilling over the edges of the short paragraphs.

In terms of content, you'll want to open the description by introducing the characters and primary conflict. If it's historical fiction, make sure we know the setting. Otherwise, your goal for **the first part of your description** is to get your main character(s) from point A to point B—from the situation they're in to open the book to the inciting incident, the first thing that really puts the plot in motion. Again, this could be one to three paragraphs, but only if those three paragraphs are short.

In the second part of the description, you'll want to describe what the character does to try to solve the primary conflict and whom they do it with. How do their goals change? How does it get harder to achieve them?

Only mention characters who are vital to the plot or add big-time fandom and intrigue, and limit the amount of names to around three or four. While we're at it, the same goes with proper nouns in general—too many of these (like City Names) and it can increase the reading difficulty, especially if the person or place is only mentioned once. Your description should be easy reading. The end of part two should also probably end with a cliffhanger. Make it propulsive to finish the whole description. But also, I wouldn't go much further in the plot than 33%.

For part three, promise the reader what they will gain by reading your book. This could be inclusion of your genre/subgenre, a keyword or two, and a catchy last line. This could also be a useful place for another blurb, either direct or infused with summary.

The only requirement for the final sentence of your description is that it is good. Get me out of there feeling like I've got to read more.

For examples of the best fiction or memoir descriptions I've worked on, visit the Amazon pages for *Return of the Fifth Horseman* by Dennis M. Clausen, *Wipe Out* by Teresa Godfrey, or *Beyond the Sunset* by Sherry Knowlton.

How to Write Descriptions for Informational Titles

Nonfiction descriptions are a different beast! But they've got a similar foundation. You should still have that bolded hook to start everything off. What's your biggest selling point? What solution to what problem do you provide? What question is your reader asking?

In part one, you'll want to introduce the reader's problem. If you've written a self-help book about improving nutrition, you'll want to describe how hard it is to know the right foods to eat because of the availability and marketability of so many bad ones. (Probably.)

In part two, you'll want to talk about the specifics of how this book solves that problem. This means analyzing the current contents of your fridge, what your body needs, and the times of day some foods are best consumed.

Part two is also a great spot for a bulleted list! Talk about scan-friendly. I've liked bulleted lists forever. It's among the first things browsers look at, and it can break down really important information concealed in your book in a straightforward way. I use one in my description on Amazon if you'd like to see an example.

For the final part, I like to end by looking into the future. What life will be like once your problem is solved. As always, your final line should be strong, catchy, and propel readers to the buy button.

For examples of some of the best nonfiction descriptions I've worked on, visit the Amazon pages of *Amelia Earhart: The Truth at Last* by Mike Campbell and *Memorable: Lessons to Leave a Legacy* by Kalyna Miletic.

How to Write Descriptions for Poetry, Short Story, and Essay Collections

You can't write about your main character in the opening paragraph if you have twelve of them. So short story collection descriptions are going to read differently than novel ones.

We're still starting with a bolded hook. Blurbs are especially effective in this slot, but if you've got a clear theme throughout the collection, you may be able to lead with that in an enticing way.

In part one of the description, you'll want to hone in on the collection's overarching theme(s) rather than one story in the collection. It could solve a problem, evoke a setting, contend with the supernatural. Help the reader understand what conversations your stories are having. If *What We Talk About When We Talk About Love* by Raymond Carver was still trying to sell more copies, the description writer would probably want to start by talking about Carver's accolades and the first paragraph could be about how love looks different on everyone.

In part two, you can get into more specifics of how those stories contend with the themes described in the first part. This means naming a story outright (using quotation marks) and introducing the character(s) and conflict(s). A second specific story could further drive the point home, and a third could deviate from the expected. You could even include all eight of your stories in the collection if you use a bulleted list and you can boil the storylines into one-line hooks.

And the final part does much of the same as the novel and nonfiction descriptions. Hammer home how the book will change the reader for having read it. Blurbs work especially well with story and poetry collections since quality is among the most important for these genres.

How to Write Shorter Descriptions for Email Pitches

In addition to writing a book description for your Amazon page, you're going to want to write a shorter one for your email pitches or (if applicable) your back cover. Sometimes you won't want to use a full description in a pitch—maybe as short as two lines—and you'll want to have perfected it before you've hit pitch time.

It will also benefit you to draft pitches from different angles: while your big book description might not focus much on the romance, if you're pitching a romance blog, you will want to pitch from that angle. The same principles apply to all the tips above—just condensed, with even fewer proper nouns.

The most important thing with book descriptions is readability.

It should be easy to understand. Make it easy on the reviewer to follow the story of the characters they barely know. When review-writing time rolls around, your informative description can show them your preferred way of describing the plot and characters so they can pinpoint how to angle their own summary.

#5. Write a semi-personalized, professional pitch letter.

I hope you get reviews without having to ask people, but you're not going to get enough of them that way—especially not right out of the gate. You have to ask.

Each pitch depends on each recipient. If you're pitching a trade review publication, they may not care much about the personalization and format of your pitch, and yet, other recipients could make their whole decision on it.

You'll want to personalize the greeting in each pitch no matter what. Throw "Dear Sir/Ma'am" out the window, please. If you can't find a name to pitch, just use the company or blog name. But the greeting isn't the only thing you'll want to personalize. If you're pitching a romance blogger for your Young Adult romantasy novel, you'll want to pay more attention to the love story in your pitch than the coming of age fantasy part. Here's what I recommend in every pitch:

- Start with a personalized greeting (preferably by name).

- Demonstrate your awareness of their reading preferences by mentioning their recent work or how you found them.

- Tell them you have a book they might be interested in with your shorter description.

- Provide a way for the recipient to learn more (either a non-Amazon webpage or press release).

- Ask directly if you can send them a copy to review.

Sample Pitch Letter

Hi [First Name],

What a pleasure it's been finding your work! Your review of [Title] shows me how much you care about fantasy and its application to real life. It's exciting to find a fellow fairy lover too.

My most recent novel [Title (publisher, release date)] is a YA romantasy about fae finding love on the brink of climate extinction. I'd love to send you a copy to check out. Here's a larger description:

[Short description]

Independent Book Review *called it **"A groundbreaking series opener with some seriously amazing teen leads,"** and* Publishers Weekly *called it **"immersive"** and **"moving on more levels than one."***

Can I send you a digital or physical copy for review on your blog and/or Amazon? Here's a little more about me [Hyperlinked landing page] in case you'd like to learn more.

-Lana Linsome

And one last thing to keep in mind: If you draft your pitch in a word processor (like Word or Pages) and then copy and paste it into your email provider (like Gmail), it could change the email font into something awkward and unnatural-looking. I usually recommend typing the whole pitch letter into your email provider with your usual font and then copying it from there for your next pitch.

#6. Craft an enticing, informative subject line.

Some review platforms request something specific in the subject line, like "Review Request: Genre + Title + Author Name." If they have those specifics on their guidelines page, definitely follow them.

If they don't—which many don't, especially the bloggers and influencers—you'll be in charge of the subject line. And you really can make it or break it right there.

Every reviewer is different. Every book is different and has different selling points. The best way to approach this would be to draft multiple subject lines.

Start with your book's best hook. That could be your tagline, an elevator pitch, a blurb you've already received, your previous recognition as an author—again, it looks different for everyone. Find out how to communicate what your book's best angle is and mention the request in the same subject line. Don't be too long either—seven or eight words is a good marker to work toward.

My favorite subject lines to receive at Independent Book Review are the ones with strong taglines or elevator pitches. I want to know quickly that the book sounds good and might offer something brand new to the market. *The Body Harvest* by Michael J. Seidlinger was pitched as "a transgressive horror novel for the TikTok generation" in the subject line. Sign us up!

Bad subject lines are usually about as vague as they come. Avoid only the words "Review request" or "Will you read my book?" Help me know what you're pitching even before you pitch.

Now let's get to some big-time difference makers: the Intangibles.

3

THE INTANGIBLES

HOW TO INCREASE YOUR CHANCES OF BEING REVIEWED (PART 2)

I ntangibles are near impossible to put a value on. They're the things that set books apart from others and also the ones that automatically count you out for some platforms. Unlike the Essentials, it's okay to not have or complete all of these, even if it can be a major boon if you're able to achieve them.

Let's talk about it.

#1. Have a good author brand and bio.

The ultimate intangible! I couldn't tell you how many times authors have admitted—their voice low over the phone—that they didn't have many social media followers. That they're not even into that kind of thing.

They're right to see it as a mark against them. It's true that reviewers like recognizing the author, whether they've read them before or can see that a lot of people already like them. The more followers on your side, the higher reviewers' blog traffic could be.

When I was pitching books for review for publishers, the authors who had name recognition always had the highest conversion rate. It's not the only reason I accept books for review at IBR, but it's definitely one of them.

That doesn't mean you have to be well known to get reviews, though. It's an intangible—a plus—but it's not the end-all be-all.

If you have a lot of followers on social media, it might even be worth linking that platform (Instagram for example) in your pitch so that they can witness your best without you bragging. If you're the bestselling author of a movie-optioned fantasy series, you're increasing your chances of getting reviewed just by using your name.

Your author bio is the first tool you'll use to convince a reader you're an author worth reading, even if you don't have a big name.

A good author bio starts with your best and doesn't include any extraneous information that doesn't have to do with your book. For example, you probably don't need to include your bachelor's in education from Generic University if you're releasing a poetry collection that doesn't deal with the classroom. I'd recommend no more than 50-75 words for the bio on Amazon and your book, while your author website bio can be longer. I like starting with your full name, your expertise or publications or accomplishments (but not a lot of them), something personal, your location, and your website.

> Rachelle Rockette is an AI entrepreneur with over 30 patents to her name, including [CompanyName] & [CompanyName]. The author of three previous books, including the bestselling [*Title*], Rachelle lives in Brookline, Massachusetts and enjoys beating her son in pickleball. Learn more at [RachelleRockette].com.

Unless requested specifically, you may choose not to include your author bio in your pitch letter. Saving the recipient's time by giving them less to read can often be a good thing.

One of my favorite ways around this is by linking your professional author website to the bottom of the pitch: "If you'd like to learn more, check out [AuthorName].com."

If you don't have a website yet, go create one. It doesn't even have to be a paid domain if you don't have the funds right now—just a well-designed look with important information, like purchase links, bio, press info, and your newsletter signup form. (Although, paying for a domain adds an extra layer of professionalism, so you should probably get it eventually.) Your website is a useful hub for readers as well as Google and AI assistants to pull from your website if someone is asking them for your exact kind of book.

If you're pitching a social media influencer on their platform, your profile takes over the role of your website. If you have a big audience on the platform you're using to pitch them, that's a bonus! The recipient could see that collaborating with you is beneficial. If you don't have a big following, just make sure you've done a good job with your content and curation on that profile so that they can trust your book as a good one.

#2. Capitalize on connections

Some review platforms—like mine!—will pay special attention to pitches from a specific indie press or a publicist. I want to review books that can sell to readers, and publicists and publishers act as a sort of quality gatekeeper for me. This person has sent me a great book in the past, so I feel like the next one could be great as well. IBR benefits when the books are good and attract attention.

The intangible part of this? If you have had a one-on-one conversation with an assigning editor at Publishers Weekly, use that connection.

If you don't, you can work to make connections. This is one of the benefits of social media. Interacting and engaging with people on their platforms—especially with social media influencers and bloggers—can go a long way in developing a relationship worthy enough to result in a review. If you've shown these people you're willing to help them, they may be more inclined to help you. But of course—it's still about the book in the end.

#3. Write in a popular genre with buzzy key-words.

You wrote the book you wanted to write. That's a good thing. But it doesn't mean it's a genre everybody wants to read.

If a publication reviews more literary fiction than poetry, they'll accept more literary books. Maybe they have more readers in that genre or they know that their audience buys more books with beautiful prose than cascading stanzas.

It's true: some books have smaller audiences than others. If you wrote a book on farm equipment, you'll have a tougher time finding reviewers than a true crime book or a family drama literary novel. So approach review-targeting with that in mind. I'd hate for you to spend too many hours trying to get the most notable platforms to cover your tiny-niche book for free.

If you wrote that farming book, definitely still target reviews—but do it mostly on Amazon and laser-specific niche blogs while putting your excess marketing time elsewhere, like participating in rural area festivals, podcasts, or getting shelved in rural bookstores.

#4. Be visible and validated before you send the pitch.

If I find a pitch in my submissions inbox for a book I've seen before, that is a good thing. Maybe it was the eye-catching book cover that flashed across my social feeds, or maybe it was someone I know reviewing it. Either way, you've got yourself a higher likelihood of getting accepted if the reviewer has that moment of recognition. It tells me this: this book could be popular or relevant to me if it found me in the algorithm.

Word of mouth is an incredibly powerful tool in marketing. If you get people to talk about your book and recommend it on their own, you're doing something right. If you needed another reason to write a book so good that people talk about it to their friends, consider this it.

I'd love it if you went viral on social media before your pitch, but it's okay if you don't too. You can still make it look like your book is being talked about regardless. If browsers can find reviews of your book on Google, social media, and Amazon at the time of the pitch, they can be influenced by it. Reviewers like it when they're reading a book that's been read by a lot of people; that means their review could get more traction and they can join an ongoing conversation. You'll have more luck pitching an influencer six months after publication if your book has more than 100 reviews on Amazon and you're intensely Googleable.

Another way to determine whether a book could be worth accepting for review is whether it recently received some acclaim, like in awards or book lists. If your book has been listed as one of the best by a cool platform like Bookriot, I'm drawn to it.

This validation can come from mentioning it outright in your pitch letter as well as just letting them research you on their own. Use the word "viral" if you actually did go viral, or you can link to your most popular platform and mention your audience or maybe how you got them. And of course, you can quote from reviews in a pitch without sounding like you're promoting too much.

If you're a debut author with limited word-of-mouth proof, you can still get reviews, but your chances aren't quite as high. This is why it's an Intangible.

#5. Your book isn't too long

Some reviewers either don't like big books (over 100k words), bigger books (over 150k words), or the biggest books (beyond), and others just don't have the time for it right now.

No matter if you're pitching a customer reviewer or a media reviewer, they'll have their preferences. In my experience, you'll get fewer reviewers with a bigger book than you will for a short or moderately sized one. Some media and trade outlets (like mine!) pay their reviewers more for bigger books, so they could take into account whether they'll spend more to cover it when choosing to accept or pass.

Size also depends on genre. Your review count might not really go down that much if you've written an epic fantasy at 130k words. Your audience expects that, so it's less important than other considerations. Write a great book with no wasted space, and your 150k word memoir will still get reviews. Just maybe not as many of them.

#6. Write a great book.

This may sound obvious, but it's a bit more nuanced than that. I want you to write the best book because I want to read the best books, but as a marketer, a good product is a top-tier intangible.

If you've done well enough in your pitch for a reviewer to open your attached or linked book, that's a great thing. Just make sure those first few pages entice them enough to keep reading.

The rest of the book matters too. Reviewers are more likely to post a review after they've finished, so they won't post a review if they never finish. Even if they do finish and didn't like it, they may choose not to post a review at all. Either they don't want to give it more time or don't want to hurt the author.

It's simple: Write a great book —> Get more reviews.

#7. You follow up with the reviewer.

I have gotten so many customer and blog reviews because of follow-up emails. Sometimes all it takes is an extra nudge to the top of the recipient's email inbox to make sure they open your pitch. I'd usually wait at least seven days before sending a follow-up.

I usually recommend only following up once. If they don't respond after your follow-up, take the hint and spend your time elsewhere.

Some follow-ups can be successful months later, instead of seven days. If you pitched six months in advance of publication, you can pop back in at two months pre-pub with updates on the blurbs and reviews you've gotten in the meantime. If that's the case, you could probably do a second follow-up right around launch time and assure them this will be your last email.

In your follow-up, make sure you don't sound like you expect the review from them. The right friendly tone can go a long way in making a reviewer interested in supporting/reading you.

Sample follow-up email:

[First Name],

Just tossing a gentle follow-up your way in case you'd like a copy of my YA romantasy! It's about fae finding love on the brink of climate extinction, and I think it could be a good fit considering how much you loved [Comp Title].

Since I last emailed you, it's gotten a STARRED review from Independent Book Review and was called "simultaneously sweet and powerful" by BookRiot. I'd love to send you a copy for a review.

Happy to answer any questions if you've got them!

-Lana

#8. Pay them.

Authors with low budgets may not like this section, but...it's true! If you can pay for book reviews, you're going to get more of them. You won't want to pay reviewers to leave reviews on Amazon (against Amazon's policy!), but you can pay for blurbs and trade reviews to add to your editorial reviews section on Amazon.

I started IBR to promote and sell indie books to readers but also because I saw the value in paid reviews as a marketer. This is the only method I know where you can guarantee blurbs and trade reviews within a certain timeframe. This way, you're giving yourself the best possible chance to use a respected company's name, their praise, and a link to share with your audience as publicity.

Remember: that doesn't mean you're paying for book sales or positive reviews; instead, for the chance to obtain blurbs and publicity.

And of course, it's optional! A way to save time pitching and to still reap the benefits of a free review. It's an Intangible. A way in.

4

BEHIND THE SCENES WITH A BOOK REVIEW PUBLISHER

I t's time to jump through your computer screen.

Go from pitcher to pitched.

Come to Panera Bread with me and watch as I receive pitches in my inbox and assign them to my team of reviewers.

The logistics of assigning book reviews

In 2024, Independent Book Review reviewed about 550 books between traditional reviews and book lists. We may have published only 350, but that was because some authors or publishers decline publication or push it off until the following year. But 550 is the number we're going to look at in this chapter. That's how many books I had to assign or read myself.

I usually manage about thirty reviewers at a time. But when your book comes across my desk, I don't have thirty reviewers to send it to.

Just from availability alone, I can usually count out about fifteen of them.

After that, I have to make my pitching decision based on the reviewers' stated interests and from what I've read of their reviews in the past. You get to know who likes which genres best from actually reading the reviews—not just asking for their genre preferences.

What I look for in a reviewer

According to our Amazon and Bookshop.org affiliate dashboards, the best-reviewed books sell better than the mixed review books. But my job is not just about sending books to people who I think will write positively about it.

If a reviewer is writing positive things only, I don't get to learn which of the books are actually the best. I want to know which books to feature in lists and social media posts because, like a book publisher, I want to focus on promoting the books that can increase sales.

That is why I look for honesty, genuine insight, story specifics, authentic fandom, and authority over subject matter in my reviewers. Being a good reviewer is about gaining readers' trust but also about truly knowing and appreciating the genre. You get more nuanced, specific, authoritative reviews when they read the genre often. I don't want sentences that unintentionally bash other books in the genre in order to compliment this one—*"Self-Help books can sometimes feel empty, but this one..."*—or use a praise paragraph to compliment a feature that's used by a lot of different authors in the genre—*"This book uniquely infuses personal memoir with self-help."* When a reviewer knows a genre well, they can better communicate what stands out about yours.

I love to see a book in our submissions inbox and to write down a reviewer's name even before I finish reading the description. I don't always get it right of course—because I didn't read the book first—but that's what our critics are for.

> # What you can learn from this

If you position your book with an Ideal Reader in mind, you make my job easier.

I love to get a book in our submissions inbox that screams a particular reviewer's name. Sometimes, I've read that reviewer over a hundred times and know that they liked this aspect in this book and that aspect in another, so when I see you've merged the two—throwing in some pop culture references to boot? I know I can send it to that reviewer, and they'll be able to write a strong review that—if the book does well—can sell books.

Not all books are easy to assign though. Sometimes the Ideal Reader is unclear. Sometimes the description is too short or the cover doesn't match the genre or the genre delineation causes a mix-up.

You can pay for reviews without a clear image of the Ideal Reader, but it makes it harder to send to the right reviewer. If a book is pitched as literary fiction, I send it to a literary reader, but if it turns out to be more of a thriller because it wasn't positioned correctly, I could get a less authoritative review.

Make it easy on me, and you've got a better chance of being placed with the right reviewer.

> # Why do I choose certain books for review?

IBR is only one platform. I am only me, a reader and a writer who cares a lot about indie authors and presses and the work they're doing. Not every platform thinks like me, but we likely have some common goals, like:

- We want to sell books and bookish things through our affiliate links.

- We want to rank high on Google so new readers and writers find us.

- We want to be a trusted resource for librarians and bookstore buyers to make their stocking decisions.

- We want to build trust with real readers, which sometimes means critiquing books that don't satisfy and highlighting the best in starred reviews and book lists.

If I am going to cater to readers and increase affiliate income over the long-run, I need readers to agree with our reviewer after they bought a book from our recommendation. If they read it and think this book really did deserve a starred review, they'll be more likely to buy something else from us in the future. As any author or publisher with some books under their belt will tell you, it's easier to convince the same reader who liked your book in the past to buy another book of yours than it is to rope a completely new reader into a first-time sale.

Truth be told—I chose a niche that is unpopular in nature. I would get more website hits and affiliate income if we ranked high on Google for our book review of *Fellowship of the Ring*, but I care less about that than other platforms. I am a writer at heart, an indie press marketer by trade, and a deep appreciator of great work in unexpected packages. I don't care very much if you're already popular.

Instead, I'm going off the power of the pitch and the enticing nature of the marketing in the free review pile—signs that you could get big down the road. Maybe we review your first or second book, and then the third one is the one that splashes. If someone hits the internet looking for more from you, they might find us.

I don't shoot for a set number of free reviews every month. But for reference, we received five hundred submissions in May 2025, and we chose twelve to review. Every month is different. My team and I choose two days out of every month to comb through submissions and find the best books. They are all over the place genre-wise, but the ones who are doing it right are clear from the beginning. We have so many submissions to get through that we don't often read the full email.

Most pitches don't need that. Close to 75% of the pitches we receive are quick rejections. Whether it's because the cover is unattractive or the pitch doesn't include something that's required, we mark the email as read and move on to the pitches that shine with Essentials and Intangibles.

Bottom line is: If your book looks like it could help me achieve all my goals, I'll be more likely to accept it for review. If your book is clear upon submission who would most enjoy it, I can get it to the right reviewer and hopefully have them nail down the specifics enough to communicate with readers of the genre that this is the one they should buy.

The truth about pitching book review publishers

Sometimes you can do everything right, and it still doesn't work. Maybe your pitch just had one fewer Intangible or struck out an important Essential. Sometimes it's just timing—my reviewer who usually loves that book just can't take it on with their current schedule. I'm usually pretty flexible for when reviews can go live so I can wait for the right book, but not all publishers are. Some review publishers need long lead-up times for that reason exactly.

Okay, now you know what you need to know about book reviews. **Let's go get them.**

Part 2: Blurbs (or Editorial reviews)

Definition: *Blurbs are short book reviews written by authors or experts in the book's field.*

5

How to Get Blurbs (or Editorial Reviews)

Like testimonials for a business, blurbs increase the validity of your product. Everything you do as an indie author to make your book appear professional and appealing helps it in the long run. You're up against giants. Why should a reader choose to spend their time reading you instead of them?

With social media, you have to post something to make it work. You might be able to tie your post to a spike in sales, but blurbs or editorial reviews do their work silently. Sitting patiently on your product page, influencing sales without you needing to do the work of snapping a picture of your face on Instagram.

In addition to influencing sales, blurbs can also influence other industry professionals like bookstore buyers, librarians, reviewers, bloggers, and audiobook producers. They work.

When I get free submissions at IBR, I look at a variety of things, including if someone like Clint Smith has said something nice about the book. If it's in the right genre and I agree that the content sounds good, I am more likely to pay my reviewer to review it.

But before you start pitching authors and experts, make sure your book is ready.

It doesn't have to be copy-edited yet—just make sure the story is in its final shape and you're proud of the characters and sentences. You can tell your hopeful blurber that the book hasn't been copy-edited yet after they accept your blurb request.

I'd recommend setting a goal of obtaining at least five blurbs one month before launch day.

Who do you ask to blurb your book?

It depends on your genre, but here are some options:

- Authors in your genre or niche

- Professional reviewers (Independent Book Review, Foreword Reviews, Kirkus, etc.)

- Industry leaders (like non-profit and organization directors in your niche)

- Professors and academics in your niche (usually for nonfiction)

Got any ideas yet?

It's time to start your book review targeting spreadsheet. You'll use it throughout this book, so don't skip this step. You can either open Google Sheets or Microsoft Excel and start from scratch, or you can grab my free review targeting spreadsheet by signing up for my newsletter at IndependentBookReview.com/WriteIndie.

Label that first sheet "Blurbs" or "Blurbers."

In the first column, write the header "Name" and list all of the people you can think of that might apply as an author or expert in your niche. Dream big with your blurber list. The bigger the name, the better the blurb. (But be aware of your good ol' writerly friend Rejection of course.)

Be sure to include authors or experts below that "dream-big" stature too. These people are probably awesome and their books are probably awesome too, but you usually know when an author isn't so popular that they have trouble keeping up with fan mail. Just like with college applications, it's usually good to have some backups.

In column two, add the person's qualification (like the title of a recent book), and, in column three, add their contact information. Email is best, but if you've interacted with these people on social media before, you *may* be able to contact them via direct message. You can usually find their preferred way to be contacted on their websites or social media.

I'd recommend having about fifteen hopeful blurbers to start. If you can't get there, I'll help you.

Put your research pants on.

How do you find blurbers?

Start with your genre. When you publish your book on Amazon, you'll be asked to choose three categories your book fits in. First, the decision is whether you're part of the Adult, Young Adult, Middle Grade, or Children's umbrella. Once you pinpoint this, you get more specific.

Since it's easiest to scroll, let's head over to the bestseller pages for a made-up book. Let's call it *Grass House:* an adult literary historical novel about a woman who revisits her childhood home after her father passes away. And little does she know, his ghost still roams the skinny, cramped halls.

Here are the genres it fits in on Amazon and the corresponding bestseller pages:

- Kindle ebooks > Literature & Fiction > Literary Fiction = <u>TinyUrl.com/LitFicBestsellers</u>

- Kindle ebooks > Literature & Fiction > Literary Fiction > Historical = <u>TinyUrl.com/LitHistoricalBestsellers</u>

- Kindle ebooks > Literature & Fiction > Genre Fiction > Family Life = <u>TinyUrl.com/FamilyLifeBestsellers</u>

Do me a favor and scroll these bestseller pages. Check out the books on both the Top 100 Paid lists and then toggle over to the Free bestseller lists.

Some of the authors who show up on this bestseller list could be out of your league or not alive anymore. Guess what? You don't have to write those people down in your spreadsheet.

But some books have just arrived on those bestseller lists—a spike in sales due to advertising or launch or some luck of the algorithm—and the author could be a good match. Write the authors down in your list, their book titles, and their contact information.

Good news is: Some authors are looking for books to blurb. You will be offering to put their name and their most recent title all over your marketing efforts—their newsletters, social media profiles, their book covers. It's free marketing for them, just paying in their time to read.

In addition to finding blurbers on Amazon, you can also type in keywords (like "ghost stories" or "paranormal") to social media, Goodreads, and Google to find blurbers.

But genres aren't the only way you can find them. Don't forget about the local angle or an alumni angle. For nonfiction, you've also got museum curators, professors, and leaders in your niche to request blurbs from. A personal connection goes a long way with procuring blurbs.

But don't send anything yet!

Look at your list. Read each one of them and realize that each one is a human, and you are about to request that they do work for you.

Yes, your book rules, I agree, but it's important to recognize that reading takes literal hours to do and that writing a blurb takes time too. You're going to want to be patient and understanding going in. Don't come at this coldly; be a friend, a good literary citizen.

How do you ask someone to blurb your book?

This is such an anxiety-riddled thing. Asking people you admire to do work for you is not easy and quite humbling. But if you're pitching someone, this is exactly what you (or your publicist) would do—you'd ask.

In an email or direct message (if appropriate), make sure you keep your pitch personal. Call them by their name. Tell them how you know them. If they mean a lot to you as an author, let them know (briefly). Don't lie and say you've read and loved their book if you haven't, but if you have, feel free to get specific. You may even benefit from taking the time to read the book just so you can approach it from this well-respected angle.

After that introductory paragraph, you'd ask them if they'd be interested in writing a blurb for your book in [x amount of time]. I usually like five weeks, with a buffer of when you *really* need it at like eight.

Following the ask, I'd recommend adding a very short description of your book with genre denominations; they'll want to be connected to the genre if they're going to read and vouch for it.

Also, if they have a book that just came out or is forthcoming, you can offer to blurb theirs back, but know your audience. If you're telling Stephen King that you'll blurb his book for him, I don't know if he'll care that much.

If you want to promise one or two blurbers actual book cover space, you can definitely do that. That may actually help convert them into saying yes. But don't promise it to everybody right off the bat or your book cover is going to be a smorgasbord with too many cheeses.

One way to increase your chances of converting with a major blurber—say, the person you want the most, whose name could help get your book into bookstores everywhere—you can give them examples of blurbs they could write. You can add a section in the second half of your pitch that outlines about three: "Revelatory! Finally someone's speaking the truth on [topic]." Or "A perspective-shattering alternate universe novel with big-hearted characters in dire situations." This is a tough line to walk because you always want to avoid braggadocio in your pitches, but it's true that some blurbers who don't have time may actually take you up on a specific quote or two, or at least use it to draft their own.

I'd recommend only sending about five blurb pitches at a time, top of the list to the bottom.

What if you don't get enough blurbs by launch time?

Take a look at book review companies.

You can request a review for free from companies like Independent Book Review and Midwest Book Review. You (or your publicist) would request a review by following their submission guidelines, and then you'd cross your fingers and hope for the best.

Or, for those with a budget, you can pay these companies to review your book. Not a guaranteed good review. Just an honest one, with hopefully a quote or two you could use as a blurb on your marketing material.

Many of these companies pay their writers to cover a range of popular books to make sure those platforms remain important to readers. Reading takes real-life time; you're paying for theirs. Not to mention their eye and experience.

Do you have to? Do you need a budget for pitching blurbers? Nope!

In book marketing, always do what you feel comfortable doing. Especially when it comes to your budget.

Some people are all gung-ho about never paying for reviews. That's fine. I actually agree when it comes to customer reviews on Amazon & Goodreads. But blurbs and media/trade reviews are a different animal. They are a way in when it feels like there is no way in.

When you guarantee a review by paying for it, you don't have to pitch and *hope* for your book to be reviewed in a certain amount of time. You'll save time researching and pitching blurbers, and you can guarantee that a reader from that company's team will read, assess, and provide an honest review of your work. Not only might you get a blurb or two, but you could also learn something tangible about how your book is being received by real readers.

Five websites that offer guaranteed editorial reviews

- IndependentBookReview.com – $$

- IndieReader.com - $$$

- Booklife.com - $$$

- KirkusReviews.com - $$$$

- ForewordReviews.com - $$$$$

Should you pursue blurbs after publication?

If you haven't gotten five blurbs by publication time, you should keep looking. I really do think you should have those in your Amazon editorial reviews section. And you can always create some graphics about late blurbs and share them on your social or newsletter platforms.

If you already got that many, you may be better off seeking media and trade reviews from here on out and just using snippets of them as blurbs. If you make a friend with an author at a book fair or something and want to ask them for a blurb—probably electronically, later—you can do that. But you don't really have to make time for blurb seeking anymore.

Sample Blurb Pitch (Someone You Don't Know):

Subject: *Greetings from a ghost lover! And a humbling blurb request*
Hi Jacinda,

*I'm glad to have an excuse to reach out! I read your last book,
[Title], and was totally absorbed by it. There's nothing like a run-in
with a ghost in the present to inform your future. (And that Timmy &
Leah romance!)*

*It was an equal pleasure to find what might just be a book sibling to
mine! Your work is in such close connection with what I try to do with
my fiction. I just finished writing a weird little novella about ghosts in
love and think it's right in your wheelhouse.*

*Would you be interested in blurbing it? It would be huge to get an
author like you to help me promote my book. I've saved a nice spot on
the front cover if you end up liking it, but I'll also be sharing it on my
newsletter, Amazon page, and social media.*

*I'd obviously be grateful for whatever you'd have to say about my
book, but if you're looking for a time-saver, you can use one of these
quotes if you end up feeling that way about it: "Epic! This is as much
about the infinity of love as it is about the mystery of how these ghosts
can break free;" or, "A deeply felt exploration of forever love in sharp
prose and magnetic romance."*

*Let me know if you're interested, and I'll send it over! I'd love to
finalize my blurbs in about 5 weeks, but if you need more time than
that, just let me know! Willing to send it no matter what.*
-Stella Starstone

Sample Blurb Pitch (Someone You Know):

Subject: *Hey there, hi there! Would you write a blurb for my book?*

Hi [Contact First Name],

[You should always start with personal, the thing that you have dealt with together. If you're former colleagues, talk about the old days; if you met at a writer's conference, talk briefly about your trip and ask them about theirs.]

As you can probably tell from the subject line, I've got a book coming out! And I was wondering if you would be interested in writing a blurb for it. Just a few short sentences would work wonders in the lead-up to my book's publication in August. I plan on using the blurb (with your name & [Book Title]) on graphics, social media, a press release, and whatever else I can think of.

It's a haunted school story about a group of teens who need to help ghosts from the school's past pass over, or they'll be stuck in school forever. Would you want to blurb it? I've got a PDF or EPUB ready if you are.

And of course—totally optional! Feel free to take it or leave it. I'm grateful for the excuse to reach out regardless.

-Tommy Tommerson

How to Recognize a Strong Blurb

1. The blurb has **at least one praise-worthy buzzword** and no more than four.

2. It comes from **a notable author, expert, or platform**.

3. **It is not too long.** (Front cover 1-8 words; Back cover 8-20 words; Amazon editorial reviews section 8-40 words)

4. It features **specific book and story elements** that demonstrate how the book both fits in and stands apart from the crowd.

<u>Strong Blurbs:</u>

"Equal parts queer, devastating, precious, and thought-provoking, *I Keep My Exoskeletons to Myself* is an unforgettable experience, exploring what it means to be human and illuminating the healing significance of finding community in the depths of your despair." - **Andrea Marks-Joseph, Independent Book Review** (on *I Keep My Exoskeletons to Myself* by Marisa Crane)

"*The Peril of Remembering Nice Things* is a powerful memoir reminding us to find the truth in our stories when both history and memory fail us." - **Samantha Hui, In-**

dependent Book Review (on *The Peril of Remembering Nice Things* by Jeffrey Wade Gibbs)

"A masterful story of grief, love, and hard work" – Elizabeth Zender, Independent Book Review (on *A Thousand Tiny Stitches* by Stephanie Claypool)

<u>Weak Blurbs:</u>

"A compelling read that's easy to enjoy from start to finish"
- **Blurby Blurberson, *Fake Publication***

"A novel with an intriguing premise and good plot" -
Blurbette Blurberson, *Fake Publication*

6

HOW TO USE BLURBS (OR WHERE TO PUT THEM)

B lurbs or editorial reviews are primarily for your use.

Sure, your blurber could post their review on their own social media or website, but it's what you do with the blurb that matters most.

The first step will always be to recognize the quality of the blurb you've received. Using the tips from the previous page, ask yourself some questions, like:

> *Did the blurber love the book and it shows, or did they share some vague or underwhelming buzzwords?*

Or

> *Are they a top-tier blurber or someone a bit lower down your hopeful blurber totem pole?*

Both of these scenarios will determine where and how often you use certain blurbs.

This chapter will give you thirteen places you can put your blurbs—your best and the rest—so that prospective buyers can see the review and let it influence their decision to buy your book.

#1. Front or Back Cover

Pull some books off your bookshelf real quick. (If you're a Kindle minimalist, I applaud you. But also go to the bookstore real quick. It's fun, I promise). You'll see something that you probably already knew.

Quotes are on the front and back of so many new covers. The best quote from the biggest author might be on the front cover or is listed as either the top blurb in a list of three on the back.

If a quote from your review is going to be on the front cover, make sure it fits all of these criteria:

- Is a really good, non-generic quote.

- Boasts a recognizable qualifier name.

- Has the room for it.

Size is a big factor in this one. Some busier covers might only have room for one or two words while others might effectively use three horizontal lines. I much prefer shorter.

If the quotes aren't necessarily badass or if they don't add value to your incredible front cover design, put those babies on the back.

Some publishers or authors choose to put blurbs only on their back cover, underneath a header like "Praise for [Author Name]." I am not a fan of these personally because, as a reader, I want to know what the story is about, but I *am* a fan of including some of them.

The book description (or a shorter version of what goes on Amazon) is my favorite thing to put on the back cover. After that, I like a few center-aligned, color-matching, appropriately sized blurbs. If there's room for your beautiful face and impressive bio, that's third.

I know this sounds like a lot on a back cover—because it can be!—but with the right design, these three elements can look more natural than not, especially if there's an abundance of empty space on your back cover.

If you feel like you can't fit everything, just ask yourself which is more impressive: your blurbs or your author bio. For example, if you're Hilary Duff, use the bio & photo. If you're Tommy Tommerson, the high school English teacher from Iowa who has a kind of unprofessional author photo, I'd recommend including the quote from IBR saying that this book was so breathtaking they needed chamomile.

The format usually looks like this, with the blurb font matching the book description font and color while the attribution could be bolded and/or capitalized.

"This book rules." - **Joe Walters, author of *The Truth About Book Reviews***

If someone is scanning the back cover, they should be able to see who said the quote before they read the quote itself.

And remember: don't misquote a blurber. If you need to save room and cut out extraneous language from their longer review, use an ellipsis. You can ask the blurber permission to cut something to make using the quote easier, but it should be the exact same content. Don't add praise if they didn't say it. If there is a typo or grammatical error, you can just change that on your own without their permission.

Most important of all! Get feedback on your design before it goes live.

#2. The top or bottom of your book description

Imagine real quick: this book but without headers, filled with the big block paragraphs that our college professors adored.

But that makes it kind of tough to read, doesn't it?

You're a writer. I know what you're thinking—that's a good thing! They won't skip any of that work you spent so much of your life-time writing—it's too good to miss.

But this isn't your book.

This is a page on the internet that sells your book.

And a lot of people skim paragraphs on their devices. It's easier on their eyes, or they already know some of the info, or they don't want to work that hard after a long day.

As you already know, I recommend using bold text at the beginning of your description to make it easier for the skimmers. For some authors and publishers, this bolded tagline should be the book's infectious hook. However, if you have a blurb that talks about your book better than you could, you should find a way to use it.

You could either use the short quote in its entirety or pull two or three words from the blurb to infuse with some book summary. As an author, you can't really get away with calling your quiet family novel "beautifully written," but somebody else sure could.

Here's a good example of a tagline that infuses a review quote for *Mother Doll* by Katya Apekina:

"Punctuated with Apekina's 'wry observations and wicked sense of humor' (*Los Angeles Times*), *Mother Doll* is a family epic and meditation on motherhood, immigration, identity, and war."

You can also do this with the bottom of the digital description: a full blurb, written out in its entirety, or infused with the closing lines of the description, intended to entice you to hit the buy button.

If your best selling point is your book's quality and your impressive blurbs, make it obvious at the beginning or end of your description.

You may even learn a thing or two about your best angles from your blurbs. If they're all talking about your expertise for your nonfiction book and you downplayed it in the description, you should probably listen to what the experts are saying and adjust that description.

#3. The editorial reviews section on Amazon

You can't add outside book reviews to the customer reviews section on Amazon, but you can put them on your book page. And on many devices, the place where you put it—called "Editorial Reviews" on Amazon—comes up before browsers can scroll down to the customer reviews.

If you have a book currently available for pre-order or purchase on Amazon, you can create an Amazon Author Central Account (autho r.amazon.com/). If you have a book on Amazon and haven't done this yet, go do it now. It's a portal where you can add an author bio, author photo, and blurbs to your Amazon page.

Once you're in Amazon Author Central, find "Editorial Reviews." This is where you can put your blurbs from *People*, Stephen King, and Independent Book Review.

You can put a ton of them if you really want to, but I'd advise against it. Once I found a Stephen King book that had so many editorial reviews that I couldn't make it to the customer reviews section. We get it, Steve!

For indie authors, I usually recommend around five small to moderately sized reviews in this section. Incorporate some bolded text—either the outlet/reviewer's name or the best sentences each one wrote—and proofread for errors. Hit "Save," and in a couple days, your book page will have praise and influencers on there.

If your book is distributed by Ingram Spark, Lightning Source, Independent Publishers Group, PublishDrive, or another indie-friendly distributor, you can add editorial reviews to the metadata and get them seen by bookstore buyers, librarians, and sometimes retail shoppers. This is especially effective when you get blurbs from trade review platforms and want to be shelved in bookstores.

HOW TO ADD REVIEWS TO YOUR AMAZON PAGE

Step 1. Log in to Amazon Author Central.

Step 2. Click the Books tab.

Step 3. Select your book.

Step 4. Choose Edit book details

Step 5. Click Add review.

Step 6. Input the review (with attribution).

Step 7. Bold the attribution.

Step 8. Save & review formatting.

Reviews (example):

"A super cool book..." - **[Blurber Name], author of *Novel***

"This might be the best thing I've read all year..." **- [Blurber Name], author of *Novel***

#4. Graphics on your Amazon page

Did you know that you or your publisher can put graphics on your Amazon product page? As long as your publisher used KDP to upload the book (which many do, even if they also use Ingram Spark or Draft 2 Digital), then you can take advantage of a feature called Amazon A+ Content. It even shows up before the editorial reviews section on Desktop.

You've got options for what size graphics you can add. They can be about your book's hook, about you, include a map of your fantasy universe, or—as you might have guessed—highlight some of your best blurbs.

You can either design the graphics yourself or get somebody to do it for you. There are horizontal modules, square modules, modules featuring text, and even a comparison chart for those getting all sorts of creative.

Graphics catch digital attention on social media, and the same concept works here. If you want to make sure customers are seeing the impressive things experts have said about your book, well-designed graphics in that "From the Publisher" section on your Amazon page could work wonders.

But beware! Poorly designed graphics or mediocre quotes could sway a sale. So do it well!

HOW TO ADD GRAPHICS TO YOUR AMAZON PAGE

Step 1. Log in to KDP.

Step 2. Click "Marketing."

Step 3. Find "A+ Content" & select your marketplace

Step 4. Click "Manage A+ Content."

Step 5. Name & add modules

Step 6. Upload graphics to modules.

Step 7. Apply ASIN.

Step 8. Submit for approval.

EXAMPLE
ON NEXT PAGE

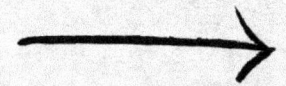

HOW TO ADD GRAPHICS TO YOUR AMAZON PAGE

(EXAMPLE)

From the Publisher:

(Source: *Criminal Beware* by Joseph Stone)

#5. Pitch letters

Blurbs can play a key role in getting more reviews and getting shelved in bookstores and libraries. Reviewer to reviewer—they work a special kind of magic.

When I see that Kevin Wilson, author of the quirky and weird and heartfelt *Nothing to See Here*, has said something nice about a book I'm being pitched, I recognize that the book could be similar in tone, feel, or content to some of Wilson's fiction. "Literary fiction" is a broad umbrella, but when you put his name next to it, I understand it a little bit more. And plus—if you could wow Kevin Wilson, there's a pretty good chance you could wow me and my reviewers too.

The same goes with bookstore and library pitches. This is a less-often used tactic for self-published authors, but it's been a staple in the traditional publishing world for ages. In essence, you email a library or bookstore asking if they'd like to shelve your book at their location. They usually need a 40-55% discount and the publisher must accept full-refund returns.

Some bookstores and libraries are deeply connected with trade review publications—Library Journal, Booklist, Bookpage—and favor books with reviews from those platforms. Some might even require it. If you get blurbs from them, you should try to get shelved in relevant bookstores and libraries.

So how do you do it?

In the following examples, I'll infuse blurbs within body paragraphs. The goal is to continue the flow of the sentence while letting your blurbs speak for you.

Sample Media Pitch (with Blurb):

Subject: *"A weirdly accurate reimagining of the first song ever played" - [Popular Music Magazine] | Review Request*

Hi [Contact or Institution Name],

My rock & roll fantasy [Title] *(June 2025) was just called **"Magnificent! A life-changing book about the ever-evolving influence of music"** and **"An epic and weirdly accurate reimagining of the first song ever played"** by* [Popular Music Magazine].

Would you like a copy of [Title] for review or feature? Here's a brief description:

[Approximately 50-75 word description]

If you want to get to know me and my work, here's a landing page[hyperlinked] *with the full description, more blurbs, and interview questions. The book is set to launch June 30, 2025, and we have both digital & print copies available.*

If you have any questions or concerns, let me know!

-Tommy Tommerson

Sample Bookstore Pitch (with Blurb):

Subject: *Tenacious D meets Men in Black in this alien-infested rock fest | Shelving Query*

Hi [Contact or Institution Name],

*My rock & roll fantasy [Title] (June 2025) was just called **"A head-banger of an alien invasion novel"** in a starred review by Booklist and **"rhythmic & absolutely absurd"** by Library Journal.*

Would you be interested in carrying a few copies at your bookshop? I'll be doing a local promotional tour in June with a launch at [Coffee Shop], and I'd love to point my audience toward your business.

If you want to get to know me and my work, here's a landing page[hyperlinked] with the full description, more blurbs, ISBN, release date, and interview questions. We have both digital & print copies available for review, and we accept returns through Ingram.

If you have any questions or concerns, let me know!

-Tommy Tommerson

#6. Social media posts

You just got a blurb you're super proud of! It turns out: Maybe you did write a good book after all. Is now the time to shout it from the rooftops?

Sure! But don't do it online yet. (And be safe up there.)

Send your biggest, loudest thank you to your blurber, add the quote to your review targeting spreadsheet, and then ask yourself these three questions:

- Will you design a graphic or video for it?

- Will you post a picture of yourself or something else personal and add the blurb to the body of the post?

- Will you post all of your blurbs during the same week in a promotional push or spread them out as they come in?

All of these are valid options. You just have to make the decision you believe in and follow through on it the best way you can.

I usually steer clear of adding a buy or pre-order link with blurb-related social posts. Followers can find your links on your profile if they like your post, and, without a link, it can feel less sales-y. But I've also read and talked to marketers who feel the exact opposite—that all promotional posts should come with a link. We're all just out here experimenting, learning, and personalizing to our own brands. Join the club. We're all the confused John Travolta meme here.

One under-the-radar thing I like about Instagram is that you pin select posts to the top of your profile and create story highlights, so your best posts or stories don't disappear. If users find their way to your profile, they can be met with your best. Blurb graphics work great in those.

#7. Email campaigns

If you have an author newsletter—which I'd recommend!—blurbs can work great in landing pages, reader magnets, welcome automations, and one-off campaigns. But since that probably sounds like a bunch of hoopla to non-email people, here's a quick breakdown:

- **Landing page**

  ○ You're going to want to design a landing page for your newsletter. It's a static webpage where a visitor is given the option to sign-up and nothing else is clickable on the page. You can explain how often the newsletter goes out, what the freebie is (if you have one), and if it's relevant to the newsletter, you can include an "About the Book" section that features a tagline and your best blurb.

- **Reader magnet (or freebie)**

  - Many newsletters offer an incentive for those who sign up for their email list. This could be a free short story, a free business guide, a free list of book review platforms (cough, cough), a discount, and more. If you send them a PDF, you can promote your book within the PDF, especially on the last page, and you can use a blurb to do it.

- **Welcome automations**

  - Perhaps the most influential tool to an email marketer! When a new person subscribes to your email, you can make it so they will be sent three-to-five scheduled pre-designed emails. If your first email outlines what this newsletter will do for its readers and the second email introduces the writer of the emails, then the third or fourth could pitch your book, which can feature blurbs.

- **Campaign announcement**

  - A campaign is just a fancy way of saying an email. For example, you write it and design it and send it to your list every other Monday. You're always looking for new content, and blurbs are great for new content. You can write about how it made you feel, where you were when you read it, or how your dog responded when you told them the good news. Consider a subject line like, "You won't believe what [Author Name] just said about [Title]."

#8. Header photos on social media

If you're being active on social media, you'd love it if somebody saw your post that included your book link and bought the book from you right then. But it's not easy to rope a complete stranger into a random purchase with one incredible post.

A lot of people visit your profile instead. So make that profile badass with impressive or funny stuff in your bio, a link to your website, and an eye-catching cover photo (if applicable). Everything depends on the style/tone on your social media of course, but I like well-designed header photos that sell your book in non-pushy, enticing ways.

I'd say you can't go wrong with your cover and a review or a few of them on your cover photo, but you can go wrong if you do it badly. So take your time with it. I've got loads of tips coming in Chapter 20 for designing graphics so feel free to wait until after you've finished there to get started. The main idea would be to include your cover, a review or multiple, and match your platform's cover photo dimensions.

Cover Photo (Example)

(Source: Facebook.com/asftrabble)

#9. Your website

Websites are beneficial in a lot of ways. From capturing emails to being a hub of your best graphics and links, the positives are kind of endless. They can even be free.

I'd recommend buying a domain eventually—it's much more professional to link to [AuthorName].com rather than a [AuthorName].wordpress.com—but the financially strapped can still design a workable free one with either Wordpress or Wix.

Just like businesses have testimonials on their websites, you should have reviews on yours. But not just thrown in all willy-nilly. I particularly like using the logo or picture of the company beside or above the quote, like you'd see in business testimonials. You can also create a "News" or "In the News" or "Reviews" page, sharing the blurb and, if applicable, a link to the full review.

Depending on your website theme, I can even see a world where you use an eye-catching static photo on a webpage that highlights your book(s) and accomplishments like reviews and the cover.

Website (Example)

*(Source: **DannyGoodman.me/Amerikaland**)*

#10. Kindle lockscreen ads

When your phone isn't being used, it goes black. When your Kindle isn't being used, there's a picture on it. And a lot of the time, it's someone's book. And that someone's book could be yours.

Not only can your book cover be on there, but you can also add some text to the ad if you want, underneath the cover and above the "Read Now" button. With this text, you can use a blurb or the catchiest part of your hook.

Just a couple years ago, small press authors could not advertise on Amazon without going through their publisher. And not all publishers wanted to pay for advertising or ask for payment from authors to cover the advertising they wanted to do. It was messy to have to go through them. Now everyone can advertise through their Amazon Author Central account. Your advertising options on Amazon are:

- **Sponsored Products**

  - Climb up the Amazon search engine when someone types in a good keyword.

- **Sponsored Brands**

  - Best for those who have published multiple books and want their face, bio, and titles to be front and center when customers type in certain keywords.

- **Lockscreen Ads (US only)**

  - For all!

I recommend testing the waters of multiple styles of lockscreen ad design, like highlighting different blurbs or using variations of your hook. I wouldn't recommend this for all authors as I've received varying, sometimes bad returns, but certain books with more flexible budgets may find it works for them.

I especially like lockscreen ads when your book is signed up on Kindle Unlimited (KU). KU readers use their device as a sort of subscription library; they pay a monthly fee and get access to all books in the program without paying more. That way, they can try reading multiple until one sticks. If your book is on KU and they're a KU user who finds your book interesting, the reader loses no money by clicking to read more.

Kindle Lockscreen Ad (Example):

#11. One or two pages of "Advance Praise" in your book

Do you have three to five paragraph-length blurbs that you want everyone to see? You can add a page at the beginning of your book—like the actual first page—so that browsers who want to read a sample online or flip it open in a bookstore will find them. It could be praise for this book, a previous book, or you as an author. No matter what, it should fill up the whole page, and it should include a centered heading like, "Advance Praise for [*Title*]" or "Praise for [Author.]"

Make sure the blurbs are good and that it's formatted in a professional way. I recommend centering the heading, left-aligning the quote, and then right-aligning the bolded blurber name and their qualification. Adding a page (or even two) like this is also one of my favorite ways to get a good review, which I'll talk more about in Chapter 23.

#12. Bookmarks, posters, and in-person promotional material

Are you planning on doing any in-person marketing? You could participate in readings, signings, conferences, fairs, and workshops. In those cases, you'll always want to have books handy, but presentation at events like fairs and signings are essential. You won't want to be there with a bottle of water and a stack of books on an empty white table. Presentation matters.

Some authors and publishers combat this with a poster or banner to capture their attention. You can definitely add a blurb or two on posters and banners.

You could also go smaller than that. Business cards should probably be left strictly to business books, but personalized bookmarks can be used by almost every author and publisher. It's a reader tool—not a business card with contact information. Make it look awesome and let people take them as freebies for coming up to your table. On that bookmark, you can leave space to feature a blurb or two, depending on the design style, like we did for Ryan Schuette's A King Without a Crown series (example on next page).

Bookmark (Example)

(Source: A King Without a Crown series by Ryan Schuette)

#13. Your author bio

This one isn't for everyone!

For those who have received an especially impressive blurb or received a particularly strong accolade like a Starred Review, you could find a way to mention it in your author bio naturally.

Sometimes the book title needs clarifying anyway, so a very short snippet of a blurb (five words MAX) not only clarifies what it's about but can mention how you did it well.

In her chapbook *Nerve: Unlearning Workshop Ableism to Develop Your Disabled Writing Practice*, Sarah Fawn Montgomery does a good job of this in the very first sentence of her bio:

> "Sarah Fawn Montgomery is the author of *Quite Mad: An American Pharma Memoir*, which The Paris Review describes as "The wakeup call we need..." She is also the author of *Halfway from Home*, winner of a Nautilus Book Award for lyric prose, and..."

7

FINDING THE TRUTH IN BLURBS

T he day you send your first blurb request is a special one. You've hit a point in your manuscript where you are proud enough to share it with readers, not just editors, and you can see a finish line. Only thing is—these aren't just readers. They might be your idols.

From the moment you hit send, your heart is going to dip a little lower in your chest. Imposter syndrome is real.

You'll think: This was a mistake. I wasn't ready for this. They're probably laughing at me right now. Your book is still in production, and you've just sent your unfinished product to someone you look up to. What were you thinking?

But truth is, all you've done is taken the step you needed to take. Believe in yourself. It's supposed to feel like this.

So send your best pitch and your best book. It could go a few different ways. Let's talk about them.

They might not answer you.

If all you hear back is crickets, it doesn't mean your book is going to tank, that it is bad, or that your author career is over before it begins. It can mean different things in different circumstances.

The first circumstance is my favorite because it has nothing to do with you. The requested blurber either doesn't check their emails or does not plan on expending time or energy blurbing anything right now. Sometimes people just aren't available, and that is totally okay. Don't feel bad. You can get blurbs from people who are. (If you feel surprised that you didn't get a response, like it's someone you know personally, maybe try a different point of contact.)

The second circumstance is that the pitch or the content doesn't match up or interest the blurber. There's no real way to tell the difference between the first and the second circumstances until some time has gone by, like months after your book is already published. Maybe your pitch wasn't highlighting what turned out to be your true best selling point, or maybe after listening to them on a podcast, you realize your content doesn't align with their views in the same way you thought it would. Maybe you did send the book too soon, and they figured out that it wasn't something they wanted to endorse, either from the description or the first few pages. All of these things are possible, but most commonly, they're usually just busy. This is a free work favor you're asking of them. Don't read too much into it.

The third is that you're not a notable author yet, and they don't trust that their blind blurb or their time spent reading, assessing, and writing about your book could be worth it for them. How can you learn from this? Well, get humble and become more notable.

In summary, if your first batch of blurbers doesn't answer you, it doesn't mean you're screwed. If your second batch doesn't answer you either, you should move even further down your hopeful blurber list.

If nobody ever answers you after twenty pitches, you are either asking too many top-tier blurbers or something might be up with your Essentials and Intangibles. If your next few review-targeting endeavors end similarly, you may want to hire a marketer to assess your Essentials and Intangibles.

> ## They answer you, but they say they are not available.

This is good news! Take away the fact that you're not getting a blurb from one of your idols and instead rejoice that you found the right contact information and wrote a pitch enticing enough to warrant a response. Some of these hopeful blurbers might even have newsletters or podcasts instead of blurbs, and so when it comes time to pitch for publicity, you'll have their contact information and a previous connection to work from.

In summary, you've done a good enough job with your content, targeting, brand, and pitch that you got a busy person to answer you. Give yourself a pat on the back and keep working.

> ## They write a blurb quickly, but it's with vague, limited, or no praise.

This is good news too, even if you did hope for something different. A blurb to use is a win, especially from an author or expert with a notable name. Sometimes with blurbs, the name matters more than what they say. Thank them for their time and definitely use the blurb (and bold their name) on your Amazon page and press release.

But if they did this, they probably didn't read your book. You did just pop into their inbox and ask them to do hours of work for you, so don't get too down about it.

What you can learn, though, is that they probably didn't have the time to commit to it but wanted to help anyway and to take advantage of the free marketing opportunity. After all, their name and title will be on your back cover now.

In the end, you're doing something right. Your content is useful and enticing simply from the pitch alone and your content seems trustworthy. They wouldn't have done this if they didn't think something was going right with your pitch.

So thank that blurber and keep chasing after the praise-filled blurb you really want.

> # They say they will read the book but never write the blurb.

This one might be the hardest to take, but it doesn't mean it's time to panic. It means that your pitch, proposed content, or your author platform were strong enough to convince them in the first place.

Your blurber could have decided against writing the blurb for any number of reasons—like they had less time to read than they expected—but it also could mean that they read some of your book and didn't want to endorse it. There's definitely something to learn from this too. Either your book wasn't ready before you pitched it, or they didn't end up feeling it was useful and endorsement-worthy. Reviews are always going to be about the content first, and no one is going to write you a critical blurb.

You should follow up with the agreed blurber in about four or five weeks (if that's what you said in the original email), but if they don't answer that email, they might be bowing out from the agreement. You can send a second follow-up a week or so later if you'd like. As long as you have the right tone, you're not pestering them with a single follow-up on a thing they agreed on, but definitely stop after one follow-up. If they don't want to write a blurb for your book, for whatever reason, they don't have to (Definitely don't ask for feedback either.) Let them go.

What can you learn from this? Well, something! Combine this knowledge with what you learn from other review targeting processes (both media and customer reviews), and start figuring out if there's something off about your content or marketing. Unless they're your editor, don't let one opinion dissuade you from having confidence and doing the best you can.

> # They write you a praise-filled blurb weeks after your pitch.

Party! Have yourself a snack. Write them back with big gratitude and relish the good review. And allow yourself the time and headspace to actually believe it. This is great news. Rewarding in multiple ways. Be proud because you deserve it, and keep it in mind as you grow your author career.

Just like you can learn about your career from bad or no reviews, you can also learn from your best ones. A great blurb from a great expert is a powerful, emotional, moving way to find out that, "Hey, maybe I am doing this thing right."

PART 3: MEDIA AND TRADE REVIEWS

Definition: Media reviews are reviews in the media. Trade reviews are reviews from book-specific platforms.

8

HOW TO FIND MEDIA AND TRADE REVIEWERS

M edia and trade reviews can sell you books, increase your chances of being shelved in bookstores and libraries, and increase your reach.

As of today, you have a set number of followers on social media and subscribers to your newsletter. When you post stuff, you hope that this content is shared to a wider audience via social media and your numbers grow, but for the most part, your content is being seen (and sometimes shared) by the same people.

When you are reviewed on a media platform, you are tapping into that platform's audience. If you are trying to reach Johnny Tucson—that dude who loves your exact kind of book in Arizona—you would benefit from appearing on a media platform he engages with.

Maybe he's a reader of The Millions. Of *The Flyfisher*. Of Independent Book Review because he loves to read and support indie authors. Or maybe he listens to a certain podcast, watches a specific YouTube channel for your kind of people. Maybe he's in a perpetual BookTok loop. He might not be in your bubble now, but after a review or feature on the right platform, he could be.

The benefit of the right media or trade review can be astronomical. You could do a great job in a YouTube interview with a popular influencer, increase your audience by game-changing numbers, and then get invited back.

About seven months prior to publication, you can start finding them—big and small, media and trade, digital and print and audio. That's what this chapter is all about: using keywords and comparable books to find media reviewers and organizing what you find in your book review targeting spreadsheet. In the next chapter, we'll take a look at the five types of platforms you'll find and then how to pitch them.

Use keywords and categories to find media.

For all you tech-allergic grandpas out there, don't worry: The terms "keywords" and "categories" are simple. And you'll need them to publish anyway, so double points to you.

Keywords are search terms that browsers use to find what they're looking for on the internet. If I wanted to learn about drawing, I might type "drawing tips for beginners" into Google. In this section, I'll be teaching you which types of phrases to type in to find media platforms.

Categories are your book's genres. This is both broad "Mystery, Thriller & Suspense" and laser-specific "International Crime Thriller" and "Heist."

I would love to talk to you about the best ways to choose keywords and categories when publishing—that was my job for a while!—but we're talking book reviews right now. And using keywords and categories to find reviewers on Google and other platforms is a little different than finding books on Amazon.

Amazon allows you to choose seven keywords and three categories when publishing your book, but you've got unlimited tries on Google &

social media. You might get lost in a time vortex Googling super-niche keywords, though, so give yourself a starting number. I'll say twenty keywords to start.

Let's make up a fake book real quick. I don't know what it's called, but it's a literary mystery about a ghost drug dealer who floats across the country selling weed to make enough gold doubloons to cross over. Since it's January and this fake book is coming out in August, we can start researching.

In this scenario, you've already got your review targeting spreadsheet handy so you don't have to spend time before researching to create an organizational file. If you've signed up for my newsletter, you've already got fifteen or so platforms to pitch. Now let's get to fifty.

I'm heading to Google first. For fiction (and this fake example), you'll see that many keywords and categories intermingle; fiction readers type in categories to find their preferred books, while nonfiction readers won't type in "self-help" so much as they'll type in something more specific like, "living with ADHD." I'm just going to get the obvious ones out of the way first, followed by the more niche.

20 Keywords to Find Media Reviews for My Made-up Literary Ghost Story

Book review sites, book reviews, indie book reviews, literary fiction book reviews, ghost fiction book reviews, mystery book reviews, paranormal mystery book reviews, small town mystery book reviews, murder mystery book reviews, humor fiction book reviews, action & adventure book reviews, supernatural mystery book reviews, psychological thriller book reviews, crime book reviews, twisty thriller book, literary ghost fiction, adventure fiction, funny mystery, Ohio book reviews, road trip fiction.

As I'm searching, I'm refining. Each search is different; each response by Google is too. If I'm not given book review platforms on page one but instead books to buy on Google, I'm adding detail to my searches or using synonyms. "Funny mystery" might give us movies and tv shows to watch, so maybe I add "book reviews" to it. Maybe I add "Novel." Maybe I use "Humor mystery" instead. I should leave each keyword search with at least one (but probably multiple) platforms to reach out to.

You can get as specific and niche with your keywords as you want. You'll want to add outlets that review your kind of books and outlets who don't review many books as well. If they're not interested in a traditional review, they could do interviews or guest posts, and you definitely shouldn't leave them off the list if they have a substantial following or are your exact kind of audience.

Some search terms will give you more platforms to write down than others. For example, you're going to find lists of book review platforms to write down when you search "book review sites," not just the two blogs you found with "psychological thriller book reviews." Oftentimes platforms that appear on big lists like these are pitched a ton of books—every other author can find them too—so that's why it's important to add them *and* go deeper into the specifics.

You should find fifty+ platforms from these first twenty keywords alone. But guess what? Google is only your first source. There are multiple search engines, there are open AI searches you can do, and you can search social media too: YouTube, Instagram, and podcast platforms. The searches can feel endless for some books.

When you do find a platform, you'll add the following information to your book review targeting spreadsheet:

- Contact or platform name

- Website (link)

- Submission Info (link)

- Submission deadline

- Keyword/Niche (How you found them)

- Pitch angle (Blurb, hook, comp books, etc.)

- Contact info (email)

- Pitch (date)

- Follow-up (date)

I just gave you a bunch of time to spend getting media reviews. Your brain's probably getting hoppy thinking about getting it all done, but guess what? If you want the most reviews possible, you should do even more. It might be time-consuming work to do all of this, but it's time worth spending.

Search using comparable titles to yours

Comparable or comp titles are books that share similarities to yours, preferably published within the last ten years. Whether it be sales, acclaim, or number of reviews, you'll want to choose ones that have achieved some form of success. For example, the comp titles for my weed-dealing ghost story could be *It Lasts Forever and Then It's Over* by Anne de Marcken, *The Orange Eats Creeps* by Grace Krilanovich, or something by Kelly Link. Overly popular books like *Lincoln in the Bardo* might fit, but they're not my favorite comp titles because people review those books because they're written by George Saunders, not necessarily because they love funny ghosts.

Even if you've written a wholly original book that defies genre expectations, other books have done that too. Other reviewers have covered those books. It's just a matter of figuring out which ones do and who's been talking about it on the internet. Comp titles are wonderful marketing tools, so I'd recommend using them.

If you don't read a lot of contemporary work similar to yours, maybe it's time to start. But even if you don't read your comp titles, you can still find them.

Go to the bestseller pages of your genres on Amazon. Here's the one for ghost fiction: <u>TinyUrl.com/Ghost Fiction</u>.

Click over to your genre(s) and jot down the titles that have similarities to yours, especially in regards to tone and description. Focus on those that have a high review count and low bestseller ranking (found in "Product Details" on their book page), and jot them down in the "Comp Titles" section of your review targeting spreadsheet.

Now that you have your comp titles, search the title, author, and "[*Title*] book review" on Google and social media. You'll find platforms who have reviewed that book, and you can add them to your spreadsheet. I also like mentioning their review of that title as reference for why you're reaching out in your pitch. "I loved your review of *It Lasts Forever and Then It's Over*! Would you like to take a look at my funny weed-dealing ghost story?"

By the end of your searches, you've got plenty of people to reach out to. Could be near or over 100 at this point. That's great news. But before you go pitching them, let's do some quick maintenance.

Make sure they can find you.

You might be surprised to hear this, but I love it when I'm not actively working and something good happens anyway. Sometimes you've been doing so well that media platforms find you. Just make sure they can. Add up-to-date contact information to your author website. You can make it a contact form if you prefer privacy, but I usually recommend a direct email just in case the form ever goes down or has a hiccup.

9

WHAT YOU'LL FIND: THE 5 TYPES OF MEDIA REVIEWS

The more you know about your potential reviewer list, the more balanced your list becomes. You don't want to pitch twenty-five trade reviewers and only two non-book-specific platforms just because your keyword and category research gave them to you first.

Even if you feel like you have enough platforms to pitch, you'll probably benefit from even more. Fifteen reviews out of one-hundred is pretty good, but thirty out of two-hundred is even better.

In my review targeting spreadsheet, under the "Media & Reviews" tab, you'll see I've separated the five types of reviewers you'll find. The better you're organized, the more clearly you'll be able to personalize your pitch.

#1. Trade book reviewers

Professional book reviewers are a good place to start this list. They review the largest variety of books across genres, so most indie authors can add at least a few to their pitch list. This could be most of what you find when you search "book review sites" and "book reviews."

Either you'll discover one platform at a time—where you can then find their submission guidelines, contact info, etc.—or you'll find directories and lists of these platforms, like at Poets & Writers: PW.org/boo k_review_outlets.

You'll want to read the submission guidelines of every single trade platform you plan to pitch. If you haven't missed the deadline to submit your book for review, add these platforms to the section under "Trade Reviews." Most of them won't answer you, but since many of them review books of various genres and you've nailed the Essentials and Intangibles, you could convert on a few. It's more difficult as a self-published author than it is for a small press author (especially if they've got a distributor), but it's still possible with the right platforms.

Review publications will sometimes offer the chance of being reviewed for free or to guarantee a review by paying for it. If you're interested in that, add a link for the service to the submission guidelines column.

#2. The Big Fish

Some large platforms don't focus only on books, but they give at least some space to it. Well-known examples of this are *The New York Times, People, Washington Post,* and NPR.

Finding submission info and emails for these can be difficult. You may find this info in the footer of their websites, on a masthead page, the about page, or the contact page. Take your time and comb through them. If you find an email—preferably one they state is for submissions or in the right department—plop that thing down in your spreadsheet.

#3. Local platforms

Locals are some of my favorite places to submit!

Oftentimes they're much smaller—which do you think gets more submissions: *Doylestown Gazette* or *The New York Times*?—and they also like headlines like, "Local author to launch award-winning horror novel at the Doylestown Bookshop." They know their audience wants books like these, so you've got a better chance.

Finding submission info and emails can be a little easier for these than the majors. Just follow the same structure of checking the footer of their website first, then the Masthead, About, and Contact pages.

#4. Niche blogs and newsletters

Traditional media isn't the only media. Small blogs have grown big, and newsletters can sell more books than linkless local papers. When you're Googling, try switching up the search a little bit. Type in lesser-discussed keywords and subjects your book contends with and find those laser-specific platforms that talk about your content naturally. They may not always review books, but that bird blog could find your nonfiction book about birdwatching intriguing for their audience and accept it for review.

As for book blogs, there are thousands of them. Some are active, some are not, and some get so many submissions despite only being a team of one that they couldn't possibly review them all. All you've got to do is find them by searching Google with all the keywords you've got, the Wordpress Discover page (or equivalent), and social media. Feel free to peruse lists and directories of bloggers too, but don't spend too much time on those. Blog lists can be found by anyone, meaning small teams can get so inundated with requests that nothing really ends up getting accepted.

But the niche platforms remain an important category for indie authors. Definitely don't skip this. Add a bunch of them. Just make sure they're still active. Thirty specifically-chosen blogs or newsletters is a good number to shoot for at the beginning.

#5. Social networking sites

Some of the best media you'll get for your book won't even have its own website. Social media influencers can be powerful on large and small scales.

Search functions and hashtags enable you to find real people talking about your book's topic in real time. That means you can find reviewers on Instagram, Facebook, X, TikTok, YouTube, and more. They can be book influencers, influencers in your field, or influencers that your audience is following. You'll also find not-very-popular social media accounts by searching on there, but we'll focus on adding them when we're researching for customer reviews.

If you decide that a certain influencer is one you'd like to pitch, be part of their community for a while. Like and comment and share their content. Be real so either the influencer or their followers can recognize your name. And then pitch them. Let's talk about how.

10

HOW TO PITCH FOR MEDIA AND TRADE REVIEWS

You've got contacts. Places and people to pitch. Starry eyes from imagining your cover on their website with a star next to it or featured in a list called "The Best Mystery Thriller Books of 2025."

But that won't happen if you don't ask them. Crack your knuckles, give yourself a few hours of work time (spread out over a few days), and get pitching.

When is the right time to pitch?

As you learned in the research phase, some platforms require submissions six months in advance of publication—a tough feat for indie authors planning on capitalizing now. Those platforms might even require physical ARCs rather than digital, which you'll need more time for. Get the cover, ISBN, description, price, publication date—everything they ask for on their guidelines page.

This is one of the reasons why it can be the right move to push back your anticipated publication date. Not only can you spend time on thoroughly examining and improving the quality of your book, but you can give yourself a chance at getting these trade reviews. The more deadlines you hit, the more chances of trade reviews you get—plain and simple.

But for the platforms that don't require lead-up times, I would wait to pitch platforms until your book is one month away from being on Amazon—whether pre-order or purchase. That way, if the platform is ready to review the book in a month, they can post the link along with it. If a browser thinks a book sounds incredible after discovering a review on IndependentBookReview.com, it'd be best they have a link where they can buy it instead of reading about how good it is and not being able to buy it yet.

Short answer: Follow each platform's guidelines as a first priority. If you don't hit a deadline, don't pitch the platform. For those who don't specify deadlines, pitch them one month before the book is available for pre-order or purchase; that could be six to eight months pre-publication or around the time of publication or shortly after. Aim to make the majority of your pitches pre-publication, but keep pitching platforms for as long as the book is relevant.

How to structure your pitch letter

Pitch letters for media and trade reviews sound much different from the ones you use for blurbs. You'll need more publication info and require more professionalism than personalization. Personalization still matters, but if you know an author you want a blurb from, you're going to be more conversational in tone than with media reviewers.

Basic Pitch Letter Structure

- **Part One:** Personalize it (name & angle).

- **Part Two:** Mention your blurbs or Intangibles.

- **Part Three:** Give access to book info (cover, description, pub date, etc.).

- **Part Four:** Ask directly for a review and give access to the book.

#1. Personalization

When you can greet a recipient by name in your pitch letter, do it. (But spell it right.) Always avoid "Dear Sir/Ma'am," "Dear Editors/Reviewers," and "To Whom It May Concern." If you can't find a name, use the platform name. Make it clear you're reaching out to them specifically.

After the greeting, you won't have to personalize the whole pitch letter every time. For some trade platforms, you won't have to mention a specific book they reviewed, mention how you liked it, and talk about your book's similarities to it—that doesn't matter. Trade platforms review so many books that your Essentials and Intangibles will be considered, not the personalization of your pitch.

For most other platforms (like the Big Fish, locals, influencers, etc.), I like to personalize. The first paragraph is usually the most natural place to do that.

If this platform has reviewed and liked another book of yours, that's the one I'll always be sure to mention. If you get one book to convert, your chances of getting reviewed a second time go up. You're building a connection, and they're recognizing you as an author with validated quality. If you promoted their review the first time around—like shared or made a graphic on social media—they could recognize that you might do the work to spread the word for them: another bonus and reason to accept this book.

If you haven't been reviewed by them, you could:

- Explain how you found them and how excited you are about their newsletter.

- Talk about how and why you liked a book they reviewed.

- Mention early about your small press if they've worked with them before.

But be careful not to sound disingenuous or to overdo the personalization. Don't lie or over-exaggerate. Keep it to a sentence or two and then move on to the meat of your pitch: the blurbs, description, and request.

#2. Mention your blurbs and Intangibles

I used to worry about sending pitches to reviewers with other reviewers' praise in it. *Is this recipient tired of battling this competitor for popularity? Am I counting myself out before I begin?*

But then I started IBR. We're not jealous over here. We want to review the books that other places are reviewing; we want to know a book is good without reading it. Blurbs and outside reviews are a huge part of that.

If you got a spectacular blurb from a well-known author or you went viral on TikTok, you'll want to put that detail in either the subject line or the very first paragraph. While every pitch letter is different, one thing is constant: always lead with your best.

If you don't have stellar blurbs, point to your validated expertise on the subject matter, your award-wins or book list features, or how your self-help book is relevant to the current news cycle.

#3. Give access to book info.

Some platforms ask for specific book information in the body of the email. If they do that, follow it.

If they don't say anything other than "pitches should be sent to sub missions@independentbookreview.com," then it's up to you on what to include. I recommend the following: **author name, publisher (omit if self-published), anticipated release date/month, one to two blurbs in the natural flow of the email, genre and short description, front cover or press release attached, full PDF or EPUB file, and a landing page to learn more about the author.**

The recipient has to know what they're accepting in order to accept it. Some pitchers include a short description, their genre, and release date in the pitch itself, while others create a press release so all the recipient has to do is view an attractive file to learn more about the book. There are pros and cons of press releases that I get into in the next chapter.

Some pitchers like to use a landing page instead of a press release, which I like a lot! It's clean and doesn't require any of those pesky attachments some recipients don't want.

If you are sending the book cover as an attachment, make sure the file is not too big or too small and that the recipient hasn't requested no attachments. If your cover is too big, you run the risk of—when combined with your book file—going over the email MAX threshold of 25 mb. But also, don't make the cover a thumbnail size either. The recipient should be able to see multiple elements of your cover with clarity and, if they have to design a graphic for the review, they can add the cover without needing to stretch the file and make it blurry.

#4. Ask directly for a review and provide the book.

You'll need to ask them directly to review your book. This is important for bloggers especially, as they could get promotional emails from time to time. Make sure they know what you are asking for from the exchange: a book review or feature.

I always recommend sending a book in whichever format the reviewer prefers: physical or digital. In the world of indie books, I'll take a person who's willing to read my book for free over not getting any readers any day of the week. Of course, physical books will cost more money to print and ship, so if you don't have the budget, go ahead and offer only the ebook. You'll still get reviews, even if it's not as many.

You can include the ebook file as an attachment if the recipient requests it in full from the beginning, or you can use Dropbox or Google Drive so they can download it themselves. I usually recommend Dropbox or Google Drive links over attachments because it doesn't take up any room in the recipient's inbox and you can just copy and paste the link rather than reattaching the file every time. (Disclaimer: Don't have a live Dropbox or Google Drive link if your book is in Kindle Select.)

Proofread the pitch one final time, take the deepest breath, click send, and update your review targeting spreadsheet with the date.

Don't forget to follow up!

You are missing out on multiple book reviews if you send only one pitch. The key is in the follow-up. If you pitched at six months pre-pub, email them again three months later with an update or two, like a recent blurb or feature. You'll want to keep it short (much shorter than the original pitch) and be direct. You can either reply within the original email thread or create a new email thread; I see benefits of both, like making it clear it's a follow-up or getting a second chance to stand out in the pile with a different subject line.

You can even add a second follow-up if you pitched at six months and then three months. You can do it during or right before launch week. A publication announcement is a great excuse for a second follow-up.

If you pitched them for the first time right before or during launch week, you may want to reach out in a couple weeks instead of months. Use your relevance wisely. But don't do it too quickly! Three emails in two weeks is too many. As always, follow-ups should be gentle and understanding, never expecting.

Follow-up to Media Reviewer (Example):

Hi [Person or Platform]!

Some great news has come in since I last reached out, so I thought I'd drop in to share it.

[Title] was picked up for review by Foreword Reviews[hyperlinked to review], Independent Book Review[hyperlinked to review], and even Guitar World, which called it **"the weirdest rock and roll book on the planet,"**—*that's just what I was going for.*

Would you like a copy for review too?

11

FREQUENTLY ASKED QUESTIONS ABOUT MEDIA REVIEWS

Can I use an email service to send a bulk email instead of one email at a time?

Yes. You could save some serious time if you use an email service like Mailchimp or MailerLite to solicit reviews, but your chances of getting accepted are going to go down. That's why I don't usually recommend it.

These services can get dinged by email providers (like Gmail) and get buried in hidden inboxes (like the Promotions tab), especially if the recipient has never emailed you before or signed up to be on this list.

But if you've got tens or hundreds of books to promote, email services could free up enough time to complete the countless other marketing tasks you have to do. You could even have readers join your "Reviewers" mailing list all on their own by putting a subscribe option up on your website; not having to do research to find and add them is a big win.

You'll definitely want to use a Google Drive or Dropbox link for the PDF instead of attaching it if you're sending the email in bulk.

For indie authors with one book out every other year, **I recommend sending emails one by one.** Definitely don't carbon copy (CC) multiple reviewers on the same email. It takes more time for sure, but it frees you up to personalize your emails and to increase your chances of hitting the main inbox, not the promotions one.

Should you make a press release?

Yes! I like press releases a lot, even if I don't use them with every pitch. A press release is usually a PDF that highlights some of your book's best selling features over one or two pages. It gives you space to put your cover, description, book info, blurbs, author info, and even interview questions if you want.

For most platforms, a press release can be a nice added bonus. If it's an attractive display with an eye-popping cover and killer blurbs, it can persuade the recipient that the book will be good simply because the press release is good. So much of this is about establishing trust through good presentation. As with other aspects of marketing, if it's an ugly press release, you could hurt your chances.

I recommend making one simply because you can use it in certain cases, not because you'll want to pitch with it every time. Local platforms, in particular, are glad to receive press releases because they could choose to publish what you've written in the body of the press release. It's a chance for you to write a non-self-promotional article about what your book is about, what people are saying about it, and how it's relevant to the local audience. Save them time and clarify the marketing angle, and you're increasing your chances.

What should you put in a press release?

You can either create a one-page press release or a multi-page press kit.

In a press kit, you have the freedom to add a press announcement, the full description, blurbs, book info, interview questions, extended author bio, book club questions, and even a short sample. It should be aesthetically pleasing, using color and well-placed photographs (cover and author) in addition to delineating clear section breaks. Canva is a great resource for creating press releases, including templates.

Whether it's multiple pages or just one, the press announcement should be the first thing the viewer is greeted with. Think of it as from the perspective of a writer at the platform you're pitching. The beginning will announce the publication of the book and introduce the author and purpose for the news. Then it will describe the contents of the book—a shorter book description—followed by the reveal of when and where it will be available.

Here's the basic information reviewers expect out of a press release:

- Cover

- Author name & bio

- Blurbs

- Product details (Print length, price, ISBN)

- A sample announcement of the book's publication (see next page)

Press Release Text (Example)

FOR IMMEDIATE RELEASE

Quiettown resident draws inspiration from her experience as a first-responder in forthcoming medical thriller

(Quiettown, ID, May 2025) - Author Lennox White is a dreamer by day and a paramedic by night. Her first novel, *Beep*, is a thorough examination of the emotionally-wrought experience of saving and not saving lives as a first-responder. The surprises are non-stop.

White's protagonist, Lina Carmichael, is a first-year paramedic with a big heart and big dreams, continuously humbled by her field partner Raj Sendak. When a series of not-quite-coincidences all point to one disregarded area on the map, it appears Lina is the only one who cares.

As much as it's a thrilling investigation of a crime ring in our beloved Quiettown, Idaho, it's also a heartfelt examination of the dangers of the opioid epidemic. *Beep* is set to release in early July 2025 at Quiettown Bookstore.

After or beside the press announcement, include blurbs, author bio, and book info: ISBN, genre, release date, publisher, page count, format, price, and distributor. This may sound like a lot, but it's because that's what press releases are supposed to do: relay important information. Just make sure the design is clean and readable by using delineated sections, and you'll be in good shape. Take a look at those Canva templates and then make it your own.

Should you hire a publicist?

There is a mountain of obstacles in your way as an indie author. Just like with pretty much everything in indie publishing, you can either spend your time doing it or pay someone else to do it for you.

There are people and companies out there who work wonders for getting books reviewed by media and trade platforms. Some of those publicists have connections that you definitely don't as a first or second or third time author, and that's an Intangible that has real value.

At the same time, publicists can charge anywhere from $1,000 to over $10,000. You'll have to ask yourself: are media and trade reviews a big part of my marketing strategy? Is it better for my book than it would be to pay an assistant to target customer reviewers for me? Sometimes this is true. Some genres benefit more from major publications than the smaller ones, like those quiet literary novels that break barriers and get starred reviews, on book lists, and in libraries.

If your budget doesn't allow it right now, you and your book are going to be fine. Platforms do take chances on unknown authors without publicists, even if the chances of getting a review could be a little lower.

Like with so much of book marketing, the decision to get a publicist really does vary from book to book and situation to situation. If you think this company/publicist can succeed more than you can, while saving you some time to do other marketing tasks and writing your next book, then I say go for it. But if you only have a thousand bucks to market, don't spend it all on a publicist.

Should you print advance review copies (ARCs)?

Some publishers and authors print physical copies of books prior to publication in order to send them out for review. You can do this through KDP or Ingram. It is an expense, but if you plan to target reviews months in advance, you will only have the option to say "in your preferred format" if you have physical ARCs available.

If you wait until publication to get a physical book, you'll be crossing some platforms off your pitching list immediately and lose potential reviewers. Sending a physical ARC also could create a higher sense of obligation in a customer or blog reviewer since they know it requires money.

Still, not all platforms require lead-up times, and some are okay with digital copies. You will be okay either way, but if you've got it in your budget and have a goal of being featured in a trade outlet, you'll want to send some ARCs. You can use the back cover to share marketing information with the reviewers too, like target audiences and publicity plans. Just make sure you leave some money in your budget and some time for printing and shipping. Sending out physical review copies can be taxing work when you've got a lot of titles and you're pushing them as much as you can, so some indie presses look to distributors to handle the load and increase reach.

How is pitching for lists and interviews different from traditional reviews?

Pitching is not only about the reviews. Some platforms don't even do traditional reviews—only book lists. Others might lean toward interviews, like podcasts & YouTube.

You should definitely add these types of publicity platforms to your book review targeting spreadsheet. Sometimes, these features are better publicity than book reviews, even if they don't come with usable pull-quotes.

Book lists get good traffic—just ask my Wordpress dashboard!—and can have good search engine optimization (SEO). If someone types in "Best mystery thrillers" and your book is on a list of multiple on the first page of Google, you could get yourself some sales well beyond the publication of that list. You'll want to adjust your pitch letter to request an interview or be featured in a book list if you realize the platform you're pitching only does these types of features.

Beyond publicity, book lists are good for improving hooks and pitches. Add a moniker like "**Named One of the Best Books of 2025 by Independent Book Review**" to the top of your description or editorial reviews section, and you're in better shape than you were before.

What is a starred review and why does it matter?

Some trade publications do not do typical 1-5 star ratings like customers do. Instead, they might do "starred reviews," which is their way of delineating the best books reviewed by their company. There's a higher likelihood that the platform will promote your book in their print magazine or their newsletter if it gets a star.

The criteria for starred reviews is different for every publication, but it's usually based on being in the top 5-10% of books reviewed by their platform that year. Your book can also get this if the book feels particularly important or game-changing.

This can be a big reason why paid reviews from these platforms can be worth trying with the right budget. You may not break through review platforms' slush piles for a number of reasons, but if you believe in your book's quality, you can pay to guarantee a review and at least enter for the chance of getting a starred review.

Should you buy trade reviews?

This is a question I used to get a lot when I was working with publishers and their authors. And the answer is one I always feel weird answering. I barely buy pants.

The real answer depends on what your budget is and what your goals are. If you don't have the money to buy a review, don't buy a review. You can still get reviews without it.

But if you do have the budget for one or two guaranteed trade reviews, that can be valuable. Pitching takes time and a lot of rejection and of course runs the risk of not converting.

Paying for reviews is a way to get real, honest, (hopefully) high-quality reviews from industry professionals and to give you a better idea of how your book is being received. You can learn so much from getting trade reviews, and it can feel good to know someone who knows books read yours and either vouched for it or gave you genuine feedback based on their experience.

By paying, you also guarantee a timeline and throw your hat in the ring for book lists and starred reviews if they have them. You probably won't make your money back by paying for trade reviews (not directly anyway), but it's a wider investment than that. It's about acclaim, notoriety, recognition for bookstores and libraries, and insight into your book publishing journey.

How do you land the Big Fish?

O. People. The New York Times. Getting an organic feature in a source like these can be game-changing for a book. And they do talk about books. So how do you break through?

Personal connections give you your best shot. Know or get to know people in the right field, and you'll at least have a fighting chance to get that person's contact information and get to understand their submission preferences. This is a big reason why some indie presses can be so beneficial to publish with—same with publicists. If they've gotten features in these places in the past, they or their author likely talked to someone.

If you don't know anyone, you may be able to find staff emails on the internet. A Staff or Masthead page on the platform's website is your first option; then you'll want to visit the articles in your book's category and look for the author. Click on their profile or find them on public social media profiles like X, its variants, or Instagram. Occasionally they'll link to their websites or share their email addresses for pitches.

Keep guest posts and article contributions in mind, too. If you can write something original for a platform like that, with real genuine appeal from your expertise, it can get you the connection you seek, increase your reach, and give you a cool sentence like, "[Author's] work has appeared in *The New York Times, AGNI...*" in your bio.

The most important aspect of your pitch is to have real genuine buzz and an actually relevant story for them before the pitch. Get big on TikTok. Win a major award. Sell thousands of books. Do all the things right first, and then catch their attention. This means that you don't have to put too much pressure on yourself to even try to land the Big Fish yet.

Why do some reviews include so much summary?

It can be confusing to get a trade book review and only be able to work with a few sentences of opinion. Some platforms require reviewers to follow a company outline, like: tagline, 80% summary, 20% opinion. In a review that's 400 words, that 20% can be two sentences of opinion.

This gives you less language to use on a marketing level for sure—which is why I don't listen to that structure for IBR reviews—but summary is incredibly important for me, bookstore buyers, and librarians. Why? Because we can tell if the book would fit our audience just from the summary alone. Reviewers are subjective. Each one is different and has different taste. Their opinion does matter, but summary comes first. If a reviewer says a book is great and unique but shares a plot summary that's similar to other books in the genre, a buyer or review publisher could recognize that "unique" is only shared because the reviewer hasn't found the other books yet.

How do you get publicity around launch time?

Getting press during launch week is beneficial, but it's not every-thing. Amazon reviews, social media, newsletter mailings, and book sales should be your priorities during this time.

As an indie, your best markets for free publicity around launch time are local media platforms and lower-tier social media influencers and profiles, like your author friend and surprisingly popular cousin.

This is another reason why using a press release to pitch local media is smart; not only can you write the article for them, you can recommend the most relevant week for it to go live.

My favorite strategy for launch week publicity is actually in paid advertising. You can schedule certain things to appear during that week by paying for it. I'm thinking most about deal sites here—Bookbub, BargainBooksy, etc.—but you can also advertise on Facebook or Amazon. I usually consider "publicity" as a separate entity from advertising, but it's true that your book will show up in front of more readers (and thus publicized) with advertising during that specific launch week.

But really—the most important thing to do with reviews during launch week is to post them on social media and/or your newsletter, regardless of when they came out. You can repost a review during launch week because your followers will understand that it's the most exciting time for you.

Okay, I'm ready! Who do I pitch?

That depends! What's your genre? Who's your audience? How much time do you have before publication? You could waste hours sending pitches to the wrong people, or you could send fewer pitches to the right people. Do your research, write a compelling pitch, cross your fingers, and hit send.

10 REVIEW PLATFORMS
ALL INDIE AUTHORS
CAN PITCH

 1. IndependentBookReview.com

 2. Libraryjournal.com

 3. Bookriot.com

 4. Forewordreviews.com

 5. Publishersweekly.com

 6. Booklistonline.com

 7. Bookpage.com

 8. Bookforum.com

 9. Bookbrowse.com

 10. Readerviews.com

Access more at IndependentBookReview.com/WriteIndie

Sample Media Pitch:

Subject: *Help your teacher cross over or be stuck in school forever. | My Teacher Is a Ghost by Tommy Tommerson*

Hi [Contact or Institution Name],

My Teacher Is a Ghost *was just called* ***"A spellbinding work of middle grade paranormal horror that gives Stephen King a run for his money"*** *by Independent Book Review and* ***"an absolute pulse-pounder"*** *by USA Today Bestselling author Jim Bob Bobberson. Can I send you a copy for review?*

Here's a brief description:

[Approximately 50-75 word description]

If you want to get to know me and my work a bit, here's a landing page[hyperlinked] *with the full description and interview questions. The book is set to launch June 8, 2025, and we have both digital & print copies available.*

If you have any questions or concerns, let me know!

-Tommy Tommerson

Sample Social Media Influencer Pitch:

I'm so glad to have an excuse to reach out! I've been following you for a while now and always look forward to your book reflections. I actually tried (and loved!) [TITLE] because of you. I was wondering—would you be interested in a free copy of my book? It's got a lot of similarities to [TITLE they've reviewed], but it's got things that are unique all to itself too. It's about a magical middle schooler who needs to help his ghost teacher cross over, or he and his classmates will be stuck in school forever. Want a copy? Would love for you & your audience to see it. You can learn more about it here if you're interested: [Book landing page link].

12

HOW TO USE MEDIA AND TRADE REVIEWS

My hope: your media review sells books all on its own. My goal: to make it work overtime, regardless of how it performs on its own.

Your usage of these types of reviews is pretty similar to blurbs. Once you cut a longer review and turn into a blurb, you can use all of the strategies from Chapter 6.

In this chapter, we'll be talking about using book review links and capitalizing on the publicity provided by being reviewed in front of someone else's audience.

#1. Social media posts

Look, social media is cool, all right? I hate it, but it's cool. Especially from a marketing perspective. It has increased the amount of voices in the room, but it's also given small business owners a chance at the mic.

If you are willing to be on social media, you should probably be on social media.

When posting about your media or trade book review, you will want to be humble, thankful, and proud.

The first way to post about your review is to pull a quote from it that means the most to you and talk about how it made you feel in the body of the post. You'll also probably want to link where that media or trade review appeared so that your audience can read the full review for themselves. I also like posting links because it can make smaller reviewers glad that you're promoting their work too.

You can post about a review like that once probably. Maybe a couple times if it really blew your mind and your followers can connect with you about the surreality of receiving such good news about a project you love and gave time to. But if you post the same review more than two times, people might think you don't have any other news to talk about.

Unless you make unique content for it—like graphics or videos.

Social media is a visual tool. Sure X is still text-dependent, but I dare you to scroll two posts on there and not be greeted with a visual. Graphics and videos catch users' attention, and they can accompany your text smoothly without asking the user to leave their platform. They pause to look at it, consider adding it to their to-be-read list, and move on. If you've got followers who aren't link-clickers, a graphic is a great way to showcase the best quotes from those reviews so they remember your book and (hopefully) buy it away from their social media scrolling time.

TikTok and Instagram reels are giving me more and more reasons to want to implement more video into social media planning and strategy, so maybe give video creation a shot, highlighting a pull-quote from your review. I'd recommend Canva for those tasks, but you can also get help from graphic designers. More in Chapter 20!

Twitter/X Post (Example)

Jude Atwood (Aug 31, 2023): "I'm so thrilled! Maybe There Are Witches was reviewed in Independent Book Review today!"

Source: @JudeAtwood (X)

#2. Newsletters

There's a reason why marketers like email so much. Social media can change at any time. Twitter/X already happened. Facebook did too; your posts on your business pages used to reach a lot more followers.

Even Google has changed with their 2024 AI update. But with email, you're popping into your fan's private inbox. Something they check compulsively. And it sells books!

It takes real, time-consuming work—most things do in book publishing—but if you have a freebie, get to know your people, post regularly, and use strong automation sequences, you can foster an active, book-buying list. I'm desperate to get into how, but this is a book about book reviews. Read the Newsletter Ninja series by Tammi L. Labrecque if you haven't yet. There's a reason why book marketers like Labrecque so much too.

As you'll find out pretty quickly in my Write Indie newsletter, I like a good welcome sequence. That's four or five emails scheduled right after a subscriber hops on board. And you can start using media reviews right in that sequence. Since you'll want a good mix of promotional emails and non-promotional ones, there's flexibility in where you put your media reviews. Whenever in the sequence you're going to be pushing your recent book is where you can pair it with the cover, description, and purpose for writing it. As always, let us see your Intangibles when you have them.

But it's also more than just welcome sequences. You also want to send out regular mailings. Kind of like a social media post, except (if you're doing it right), a higher percentage of people will probably see it. You can definitely make a single mailing about a new exciting review. Even if you already posted it on social media. You can also do recent praise round-ups.

#3. Your website

I already talked about this in the blurb section, so let's keep it short.

Adding media or trade reviews to your website is equivalent to adding blurbs to your website, except now you can add a link to the review. Definitely make sure you hyperlink it or design a clickable graphic that sends the browser to the full review rather than share one of those long, ugly https://... links.

Take your favorite quote from the review, attribute it, and design it so it's easily read. Simple as that.

#4. Press releases and landing pages

If you plan on reaching out to local media, I definitely recommend designing a press release. In short, you'll want to write a short article for the platform to use while providing essential publishing information: from price to ISBN and, you guessed it, to reviews. I'd recommend using at least two of your best blurbs or media reviews directly underneath the article in a clearly separated section of its own.

A landing page is one page on the internet dedicated to either selling your book for you or accruing sign-ups to your newsletter. Since I like linking to author pages in my pitches (so I don't have to write out a full bio and elongate the pitch too much), a landing page is a good way to share everything you need to. It'll work a lot like your websites, where you provide an author photo, author bio, book(s), praise, and maybe an email sign-up form or review copy request form. Portland-based publisher Tin House Books does a great job with theirs, like this one for Paraic O'Donnell.

Landing Page (Example)

BOOKS · AUTHORS · EVENTS · WORKSHOP · PODCAST · BISHOP & WILDE   f ⊻ ◎ Q

Q ZOOM   ⬇ DOWNLOAD

VISIT AUTHOR'S WEBSITE

Paraic O'Donnell

Paraic O'Donnell is the author of *The House on Vesper Sands* and *The Maker of Swans*. He lives in Wicklow, Ireland, with his wife and two children, and can usually be found in the garden.

BOOKS BY PARAIC O'DONNELL

The Naming of the Birds
by Paraic O'Donnell

The Maker of Swans
by Paraic O'Donnell

The House on Vesper Sands
by Paraic O'Donnell

PRAISE

 O'Donnell revivifies Victorian and Gothic genre conventions,.... lyrical, clever, and evocative, rich in detail without being overstuffed... a delectable mixture of old-fashioned storytelling and contemporary verve.

—**The Adroit Journal**

 Bliss and Cutter are two of the most intriguing investigators this reviewer has encountered.

—**The Historical Novel Society**

(Source: Tinhouse.com/author/paraic-odonnell)

#5. Pitch letters

You've seen this already in my samples, but I'm a particularly big fan of using media or trade reviews in pitch letters. If it's a good platform with notable name recognition, all the better.

If you were featured in *The New York Times* for example, make sure that thing is in the first paragraph. If the quote is killer and encapsulates just what you were trying to do with the book, that's another reason to include it.

I like to add reviews in the middle of paragraphs in conversation, but you could also separate them into their own section like the example on the next page. Either way, I like bolded text to make it scan-friendly and a single link to the best review.

Sample Media Pitch (with Reviews in Post-Script):

Subject: *A paranormal thriller with an ending that's "impossible to see coming" (IBR)* | My Teacher Is a Ghost

   Body: *Hi [Contact or Institution Name],*

   Either Landon Jones helps his teacher cross over to the ghost world or he'll be stuck in school forever. My middle grade paranormal thriller, *My Teacher Is a Ghost*, is due out in August 2025, and I'd love to send you a copy for review. *Here's a brief description:*

   [Approximately 50-75 word description]

   If you want to get to know me and my work a bit more, here's a landing page[hyperlinked] *with the full description and interview questions. The book is set to launch August 30th, and we have both digital & print copies available.*

   If you have any questions or concerns, let me know!

   -Tommy

-----

   a novel by Tommy Tommerson | On Sale: August 2025 | Paperback | $14.99 | ISBN: 978000000

   "..." - **Independent Book Review**

   "..." - **Fake publication**

   "..." – **Fake publication**

13

FINDING THE TRUTH IN MEDIA REVIEWS

Y our name in lights. Or in print. Or on a website.

It's not like writers are writing for the attention. But they'd probably welcome it. They might even read a book about getting book reviews to try to get more of it.

Let's dive into the different scenarios you could encounter in media and trade review targeting and what you can learn from it.

You don't convert on any media or trade reviews.

If a few months have passed since publication and you still don't have any media or trade reviews, don't panic. You have missed some media and trade review opportunities for this book, but remember—you're playing the long game.

Book review targeting teaches you things. It's up to you to listen.

The first reason for why this happened is that you didn't hit the deadline and sent the pitch anyway. That won't work.

The second is that you pitched the wrong platforms or only the difficult-to-reach ones. *The New York Times. Washington Post. Publisher's Weekly.* They're great platforms. There's a reason why every author, publicist, or publisher reaches out to them. They're the platforms that make big differences and spike sales all on their own. It's good to shoot for the stars, but it's not wise to shoot only for the stars. Pitch the platforms that match your book's aesthetic most, but then move down the list to platforms that might not get you sales or notoriety right away. It's about getting yeses, learning what works, and repeating it (only earlier and better) for the rest of your career.

It also could mean that you didn't send a good enough pitch. If you're sending an email with no subject line and only a sentence or two in the body of the email—asking an outlet to review a book without telling them what it is and who you are—you will end up with zero media or trade reviews. But also, this could mean you're not following specified guidelines.

The fourth reason is that your cover is not working. You may not ever get this feedback even though you need it. Why? Because you might never convert reviews outside of your personal circle in the first place.

When it comes to media, they want their websites and platforms to look good, so good covers are a must. The best covers are even better, and there are a lot of them. If you even think this is a possibility, you should start making arrangements for a better cover. You can convert on media or trade book reviews if you have a good cover even if your content isn't enticing or quality.

The fifth reason is that the book description promises an uninteresting or maybe even problematic book. If your cover passes the eye test, reviewers may want to learn more about it by reading the description. If you wrote a book with very little happening in it, it will show in the book description. If you chose a topic that is especially triggering or dependent on stereotypes, you will dissuade platforms from saying yes.

And yes, that means it could be your book content that's the problem. If no one is answering you after fifty pitches and you still like the cover, you should reevaluate if it's the content that is getting in your way. That can be hard to learn, but if you really want to make a career out of this, you're going to want to get comfortable with criticism.

> # You convert on less than 5% of your media or trade pitches.

Let's say you sent 100 media and trade pitches. This includes social media influencers, bloggers, print media, podcasts, and more. First, good job. This is a great number to shoot for in your first batch because it gives you a better chance of converting but also because it helps you recognize the percentage with which you're being accepted.

If you got three media reviews out of one hundred pitches, either your pitch isn't working or your content isn't relevant or interesting enough. Read into this. Don't ignore it.

Start with your pitch. Is your description vague, confusing, or uninteresting? Is your genre wrong? Is your cover bad? Are you trying to save time by not personalizing your messages? Are you pitching the wrong email addresses? Are you pitching from a place of no authority without blurbs or an author platform? Are you pitching them at a bad time, like Saturday morning or over Christmas break? All of these are possible.

If you are getting outlets to agree but they don't actually end up writing the reviews, it could be a content problem. Many outlets and platforms these days don't like posting negative reviews, and they don't have to tell you that they're not going to review it if your book doesn't pass inspection.

Don't fret, don't sweat; you're learning. Maybe send your book out to some beta readers or editors if you haven't done that or order a paid book review from an honest platform. Find out why this could be happening, and start writing your next book.

> # You convert on more than 5% of your media or trade pitches.

It might not sound like a lot, but make sure you celebrate this. Something is working. Your pitch is probably professional and enticing, and your book is good enough to hold a reader's attention for the duration of it. You're not going to get a 50% conversion rate on review pitches. That's why it's so important to send so many of them.

Don't feel bad if you are at exactly the 5% mark, even if it is just toeing the line. It's difficult to get reviews as an indie author or an unknown press, and you're getting at least some publicity and a few more blurbs from it. Just like you read into the unsuccessful things in review targeting, you also have to read into the good. So, good job. This book might be salable after all.

> # You feel like everybody else is getting bigger reviews, and you get only small ones.

It's a trap! Run!

Comparing yourself and your book to others in the market is so hard to stop. That's why I made a fancy little section in here for you. Just as a reminder that when it happens, you shouldn't listen to it.

Connections, budget, timing, availability—this is an industry of Intangibles and ones that aren't always flexible. It doesn't mean they wrote a better book than you.

You get a mixed review of your book.

You're getting the honesty you were looking for.

A real person read your book and explained why the reading experience wasn't perfect for them. Sometimes their opinion feels unjust or factually wrong. Sometimes their opinion feels right and makes you worry. Just breathe and take it in.

Don't edit your book because of it. Just welcome that you need both editorial and review feedback if you're going to get better at this whole publishing thing.

But also, don't forget about the praise you just got too! A mixed review means getting good with the bad, so allow the good to hold the same exact weight. They mean what they said.

You get no sales after your media or trade review goes live.

Don't worry. They're all compounding. The fact that you got the review is the win in the first place. This way, you've got fodder for blurbs, a new link to show your audience, and specific, professional words written about your book. The more of these you get, the more likely you are to build a better portfolio for your audience to buy it down the line.

You get a starred review.

You'll always have this. It's powerful to put "starred review" on a blurb, whether it's on graphics, your pitch, cover, or Amazon page.

Starred reviews work differently for every company, but many of them put precedence on the quality of the content, not necessarily the salability of the book. At IBR for example, I don't care if your cover is lackluster or description is too short. If you wowed reviewers with what's inside the book, you're eligible for a starred review.

If you get one after buying an editorial book review for example, it doesn't mean everything about your marketing is working, but it does mean you did the most important thing right: write a damn good book.

Part 4: Customer Reviews (Amazon & Goodreads)

Definition: *Customer reviews are reviews from everyday people—bookish or not, usually posted on Amazon and/or Goodreads.*

14

WHAT YOU NEED TO KNOW ABOUT CUSTOMER REVIEWS

L ike any good parent, I love all book reviews equally. They do different things; they all play their part in swaying sales. But I'm going to let you in on a little secret:

If you skip getting blurbs or trade reviews, your book will survive. If you skip getting customer reviews, your book will need some resuscitation.

Customer reviews appear on your book's most important webpage: the one that sells your book. It doesn't matter how much marketing and advertising you do; if people are reaching your Amazon page and it has zero book reviews on there, you are going to lose time and money promoting and pitching.

But before we go too deep into strategies, let's get a few things clear first.

Where they'll be reviewing your book

1. Amazon

2. Goodreads

3. Other social media (Instagram, Facebook, X, etc.)

4. Barnes & Noble

5. Apple Books

6. Google Books

7. Kobo

8. Storygraph

9. LibraryThing

10. Audible

The list actually goes on. There's Bookbub, Litsy, OnlineBookClub, and more. But with how many customers and platforms there are, you can't possibly pitch them all.

If we're talking about biggest impact, Amazon is the #1 target in this section. Some people don't want to send customers to Amazon because they don't want to support Amazon, and that's cool with me. You've got other options. But for the sake of high-upside in customer review targeting, I'll discuss Amazon a lot in this section. I'll just want you to keep in mind that Amazon has different marketplaces too. If you send your ebook to a reviewer in Canada, they're probably reviewing it on Amazon.ca. It still might be worth sending them, but they won't increase your review count to 100 on Amazon.com if they do that.

There are benefits to being reviewed on all platforms. Goodreads (also owned by Amazon) is the biggest reading community on the web. If you're publishing on platforms outside of Amazon, you want to sell books on those platforms too—like Barnes and Noble, Kobo, and Apple Books. Communicate to those potential buyers that real readers, like them, are reading and enjoying your book on their platform. No matter which platforms you pursue in review targeting, give it some time but also be wary of the time lord looking to suck your hours away.

When should you get started customer review targeting?

You can start finding customer reviewers as early as six months in advance of publication. But don't pitch them until about six weeks prior to it.

Readers cannot leave reviews on Amazon until the book is available for purchase—not pre-order. So if you email someone too early (like five months in advance) and ask them to leave a review when the book does finally publish, your review numbers are going to go down; it's been too long.

I like starting to pitch at a hard six weeks because the reviewer will have enough time to read it, won't have to wait too long after finishing it to leave their review, and can leave the review during launch week—a big plus.

Locate your Amazon review link.

When you ask people to review your book, you'll want to provide the link for them to do it. When you make their jobs easier, you convert on more reviews.

Once your book is published, a specific review link is available for your book. I recommend sending that instead of the book link. To find it, you scroll down on your book page to the "Write a Customer Review" button. Click that. It will take you to a link that includes your ASIN number, the Amazon version of ISBN for ebooks. Here's what it looks like, with a placeholder for your custom ASIN:

amazon.com/review/create-review?asin=yourASINhere.

Here's the one for this book for reference:

amazon.com/review/create-review?asin=B0FD8TBQTB

> # Read the KDP guidelines on customer reviews.

There's a ton of publishing advice on social media. Facebook groups are filled with well-meaning, sometimes experienced, sometimes not, people who are willing to answer questions for you based on what they know.

But there's no better place to learn about what Amazon will let you do when seeking customer reviews than Amazon itself. Here's a brief run-down of frequently asked questions: Tinyurl.com/KDPCustomerReviewFAQ. Read it. Don't take shortcuts. Understanding this stuff is important.

As of now (and throughout their history), Amazon allows you to send people copies of your book for review as long as you don't incentivize it in some way, like paying them, sending them a gift card, or doing a review swap. You also can't ask overtly for positive reviews as opposed to honest ones or get reviews from people from within your household. It's not worth trying to get around these rules, as KDP can terminate accounts and remove reviews.

Here's an even bigger community guidelines page you should know before publishing: Tinyurl.com/ReadKDPGuidelines.

Chase the verified purchase.

Sometimes, KDP peruses product pages to find out if reviews are breaking rules. You're not allowed to share a household with someone who writes a review, for example. I've also heard that KDP doesn't want you to be Facebook friends with someone who reviews your book, but they don't state it explicitly. No matter if that's true or not, KDP can still remove reviews without much of an explanation as to why. It can be a real bummer to work for a review and then have it get removed.

That's where "verified purchase" reviews come in. When a reviewer buys or downloads the ebook on Amazon before leaving their review, they will be considered a verified purchase. It's a little golden phrase that goes underneath the reviewer's name, indicating that this person definitely read this book. These reviews very rarely get taken away, even if you're an acquaintance with this person.

That's why I like trying to get my reviewers this verified purchase tag, especially for launch team members (more on this soon!). I'm not saying reviews will definitely get removed if they don't have this tag, but Amazon runs the show. If they decide to remove all of the non-verified reviews one day, they definitely could. You don't have to dissuade your friends or relatives from leaving Amazon reviews, but they have a better chance of staying on the page when they're verified. Another plus is that verified reviews in different marketplaces (like Amazon.co.uk or Amazon.ca) can still show up on Amazon.com.

One of the best ways to get verified reviews via book review targeting is by putting the ebook up for a free promotion over two days and asking your reviewers to download the ebook before leaving their review. Your ebook is required to be in Kindle Select (exclusive to KDP) in order to run a free promotion, and it's not absolutely essential you do it, but it is something you can do to protect your reviews.

For how long should you target customer reviews?

I recommend shooting for a numeric goal rather than a timestamp. For most books, I'd say to shoot for 100 reviews. You won't be able to get that on the first research-pitch cycle, so you'll probably have to redo it and experiment with different strategies.

After 100, the only thing to do really is to keep an eye out for reviewers on social media. Pitch them when you find them and use promotion deal sites and hope readers turn into reviewers when they reach the end of your book.

It'd be great if you got to over 1,000 reviews, but usually when you see books with that many reviews, it means the book took off on its own—not man-powered review targeting.

Add your book to Goodreads early.

Unlike Amazon, you can get reviews on Goodreads prior to publication—but only if your book is on Goodreads. So get it up there. The earlier the better, but you will need an ISBN, an author website, the final cover, final title and subtitle, and a workable description. It's a lot more than it used to be.

You can add your book to the database by joining the Goodreads Librarian Group and then posting to the group following their guidelines. (You used to be able to create your whole book page on here by yourself, but now it's up to the librarians.)

You'll need your book info: author, cover, description, ISBN/ASIN, author website, and more. They ask for only a few days for your book to appear, but it's usually closer to two weeks.

Fun news of late: Goodreads ratings are now appearing on some Amazon sales pages. So even if you aren't thriving in the Amazon review department yet, you might still be able to show browsers that your book is being read and reviewed with Goodreads reviews. As of now, it's up to Amazon which product pages show their Goodreads reviews.

Add your author profile to Goodreads

Once the book is on the site, click on your author name. It will take you to a page of books written by people who share your name. If you have a unique name, it might be only your book.

At the bottom of that page, you'll find a sentence that says, "Is this you? Let us know." Click on it. That's where you can submit your author info, like author email address, website, name, and more. After you get approved, you can do more to your profile, like adding your author photo, bio, website and social links, or you can pretty it up even more with interview questions. Up to you!

Having a Goodreads author profile is helpful simply by allowing browsers to learn more about you but also for potential reviewers who might want to contact you for a copy.

Differences between Audible and Amazon reviews

Did you publish an audiobook? That's awesome. Not only is it a smart marketing decision—another product to sell!—but it's also just plain cool to hear your story read out loud by a pro. There are some core differences between Audible and Amazon reviews. Here's a quick rundown before we get started:

- Friends and family can review your audiobook. Audible even encourages it, as opposed to Amazon.

- If you publish with ACX, you get 50 free download codes: 25 in the US and 25 outside the US. So all you have to do is send a reviewer the link to the free audiobook. Then, if you get over 100 sales on Audible, you get twenty-five more codes.

- The reviewer has to listen to a good portion of the audiobook in order to review it. They'll stop them if they haven't yet.

- You can track who has listened to your audiobook codes. If it seems like they won't review it, you can send the same code to someone who will.

- Audible reviews don't go on Amazon, and vice versa. If someone bought your book on Audible, they can leave the review on Amazon as a "verified purchase," but if they got the audiobook as a gift (like the code), it won't be verified.

- It's good to have reviews on Audible, but I still put precedent on Amazon reviews. So I usually recommend authors who don't have 100 reviews yet to share the Amazon link, not Audible.

15

HOW TO GET MORE CUSTOMER REVIEWS

W hatever you do, don't skip this.

Getting customer reviews is consistent, time-consuming work, but it's time worth spending. Yes, we definitely want organic reviews to come in without having to do the work for it, but in order to make your Amazon sales page sell your book for you, you're going to have to work for that first 100.

How to get Amazon reviews was the #1 question I got from authors at the publishing houses I worked at. That made me proud. My people knew what was important. But they also asked because it turned out to be harder than they thought. They tried strategies and came away with a couple, a few, not nearly as many reviews as they'd hoped. Some of them were even good strategies.

Most of the time, this just meant that it wasn't time for them to quit yet. Customer review targeting takes real time, effort, and creativity. While it may seem like the wrong choice to spend so much time curating one-on-one reviewer relationships with non-media members, you'll see that these everyday readers can end up being your biggest cheerleaders: the ones who post about your book, share it with their friends, and sign up to review each new title you release. The time adds up, but so does the impact of reaching real people.

As much as the content of reviews matters, the numbers play an important role too. If a browser visits your book's product page, sees that a lot of people have read it and (fingers crossed) enjoyed it, then you're in good shape. If a browser visits your product page again, at some point after their initial visit, and the review count is higher, you're in even better shape. Your book looks like people are reading it right now. For one customer, that could be the thing that makes the sale.

If you feel like you're getting your ass kicked in the book review department, that's because it does that to (almost) everybody—from the biggest indies to the smallest. So strap on your metal underwear. Fight back.

Strategy #1. Ask for a review inside the book (with a link).

You're going to send emails to get Amazon reviews, but you should also get them without emailing anyone. They should read your book and review it on their own. But how do you make that happen?

The Kindle device sends a pop-up to readers after they finish reading the story, and the pop-up asks them to rate the book. Rate it, not review it. Some readers dismiss the pop-up because they want to read the bio and acknowledgements (guilty!). Also, not every reader is on Kindle.

The best way to overcome these hurdles is to add a page before the acknowledgements and bio that asks the reader directly (and kindly) to leave a review on Amazon and/or Goodreads.

I did it in my own style at the end of this book (flip to it if you dare), but on the next page is an example of one of my favorite ways to do this.

Did you like this book?

Please leave a review or rate it on Amazon at **[AuthorWebsite].com/reviewlink** or by scanning the QR code below.

I want as many people to read this thing as possible, and every single review works to help it get discovered. No matter if you loved it or didn't, an honest review will get the highest of fives from me.

-Tommy

How to Add a Link and QR code

Create the dynamic QR code first. There are a number of free dynamic QR code generators on the internet, like Hovercode.com. My first piece of advice would be to make sure it's a dynamic QR code, not a static one. This way, you'll be able to edit the link it directs to.

If you put your book up for preorder on Amazon, they'll give you the Amazon Standard Identification Number (ASIN). You'll need that to type out your Amazon leave a review link in the book. All you'd have to do is get the ASIN from the product info section on your book page and add it to the end of this string: amazon.com/review/create-review?asin=yourASINhere.

If you do not put your book up for preorder, you can still do this before publication. I like to create a redirection link; that's a link where you click on one thing (like IndependentBookReview.com/reviewlink), and it redirects you to amazon.com/review/create-review?asin=B0FD8TBQTB. But if you don't have the ASIN yet, you can send it to your Goodreads page. Then when the Amazon create-review link goes live when you publish, you switch the redirected link. Most redirection tools are available as plugins on your website or sites like TinyUrl.com. And make sure the link is clickable in your ebook!

By using this strategy, your book will ask for reviews for you. Since there are so many hours you have to put into the marketing department, I'm all for tasks that don't require more than one edit. This is one of them.

Strategy #2. Build a launch or street team.

The best way to get reviews early is to build a launch or street team. You can do this before your book comes out (preferred), during a promotion, or a randomly selected week months after publication.

A launch or street team is a group of people who agree to review your book all around the same time. You'll ask them to review the book on Amazon as a priority, but you can also get them to promote it on social media during that same week, either by engaging with your content or creating unique content for their platform.

The team is usually made up of readers you know—those who want to support you the most—but make sure all those readers aren't in the same house or share your last name, because Amazon could remove the review.

You can definitely ask a random customer you found to be on your street team, but it's usually best to cultivate a personal relationship with reviewers you don't know. That is—unless they signed up to be part of your launch team via a form, like if they found the form on your website or newsletter. Here's an example of a form that launch team members joined for this book: Tinyurl.com/arcteamform.

If all this sounds glossed over, that's because it is. There are so many specifics to cover that it needs a full chapter. "Creating a Launch or Street Team" is coming up in the next chapter.

Strategy #3. Find reviewers on social networking sites.

People are reading and writing about books all the time. If we're talking about getting reviews for the long haul, social networking sites are going to be your number one resource.

Type your book's genre and keywords into the search function on social media apps to find the people who are posting about your niche. Sometimes those people have blogs, and other times, their platform is their social media profile. Both are great for getting Amazon reviews. You should also use comparable titles to search on social media.

But it's not just about finding active accounts and cold DMing them. That could work every once in a while, but I'd recommend trying to build a relationship with those readers by engaging with their content for a while beforehand. That way, when you do finally pitch, they've seen your name and recognize you as someone who's expending their time and energy in them before you ask them to expend their own on you. And of course, the more you learn about their style, the more specific you can make your pitch.

In order, here are my favorite platforms for finding reviewers:

1. Instagram

2. Goodreads

3. Youtube

4. Facebook groups

5. X/Bluesky

Launch teams and street teams have end-dates. You won't put together endless teams to review your book all at once (though you may be able to do it a couple times), but with social networking sites, you can kind of go on pitching forever.

And while that's a ton of time to spend, you're going to want to spend it in this department. You can take breaks for sure, but if you've published your still-relevant novel two years ago, and you found a reviewer on Instagram who you haven't pitched yet, you can definitely still pitch them.

One of my favorite ways to use social networking sites for Amazon reviews is to target those users who don't have major platforms. They don't have to even post ten times on their Instagram in order to leave a review on Amazon. Publicity is a plus on social media sites, but the Amazon review is what matters most. So don't leave off the everyday users!

Strategy #4. Find them on Amazon.

Remember how we found blurbers by visiting comparable titles on Amazon?

Well, you can do the same with Amazon reviewers. Search your comp titles and find the ones that don't have 1,000 reviews. I think 50+ is a good sweet spot. Sometimes, the smaller the number the better.

Visit the product page of that title and scroll down to the customer reviews section. You'll see that some of the book's reviewers have photos and some do not, which indicates whether they've created a reviewer profile. If they have a photo, visit their profile. See if they've shared a website or social media account in the bio. There are no clickable links in their bios like there used to be, but some reviewers turn out to have public profiles and welcome free products for review.

Find them, Google their names, and add them to your review targeting spreadsheet, noting which comp title you used in the "angle" column. This is very time-consuming, but for those on the hunt, it's a direct and results-oriented process.

Strategy #5. Enroll in KDP Select and run free ebook promotions.

KDP Select is an exclusivity program that comes with both perks and downsides. If a publisher chooses to make their ebook exclusive to Amazon, meaning readers can't buy it on Barnes & Noble, Apple, or their website, they can take advantage of Amazon-specific perks.

The first perk is that you can add your book to the Kindle Unlimited (KU) library. With KU, readers pay a subscription fee every month instead of buying upfront for the price of an ebook. Since it's a large library with over 4-million titles and they get automatic access to try them out, KU readers tend to read exclusively from this library. They're already paying for it after all. So when you publish in the KU library, you share your ebook with readers who likely wouldn't have bought it otherwise.

It's beneficial from an expanding your readership standpoint, but it's also helpful when it comes to ratings and reviews. After they finish reading your book, they will get a pop-up on their Kindles asking them to rate it. Ratings can be extremely valuable since they add to your review total at the top of your Amazon product page. Did you know that if you have twenty-two ratings but only sixteen reviews, the number twenty-two appears in parentheses next to the average stars, not sixteen? It shows that number in the Amazon search engine too. Kindle Unlimited readers leave reviews too, but you often get more ratings than reviews through that library.

Another benefit to enrolling in KDP Select is that you can offer your ebook for free for five days during each 90-day period you're enrolled. This means that when someone visits your product page, they can download your ebook for free. You could technically share that free promotion with your followers and get a bunch of downloads, but I don't usually recommend that since you're trying to sell to those people.

Instead, I like to use these free download days for my launch team (more in the next chapter!) and to run advertisements in newsletters that show discounted and free ebooks to thousands of readers. As long as your book is enticing with a strong cover and description, these sites will get you downloads.

All they have is the book though. And not everyone who buys the book will remember to review it, and not everyone who downloads a free book will even read it. You did not email this reader to request a review, so you'll have to depend on the quality of your content and the page at the end of your book that requests a review. With the sheer number of downloads, you could walk away with multiple reviews because of these sites.

Some of my favorite ebook promotion sites:

1. <u>Bookbub</u>

2. <u>Bargain Booksy</u> (or FreeBooksy)

3. <u>Fussy Librarian</u>

4. <u>Robin Reads</u>

5. <u>Ereader News Today</u> (ENT)

Strategy #6. Focus on smaller bloggers and vloggers.

When you were searching for bloggers in the media review section, you probably noticed something: some bloggers have small followings.

Some have outdated, surprisingly active websites. You may have seen these and decided not to pitch them because it wouldn't be publicity you can use.

I say: Add them to your spreadsheet anyway. But put them in the customer reviewers section. Little-known bloggers and YouTubers are just people on the internet, spreading their love of books or just beginning to, and they provide their contact info and reading preferences. You've got a better chance of being reviewed by people who don't receive a ton of requests. And Amazon doesn't discriminate! A review from a little-known person sounds the same as a popular name in the customer reviews section.

In your first pitch, you'll offer to send them a book for review. If they accept the request, you thank them, send the book over in their preferred format, and say:

> *"Awesome!! Thank you, [Contact-name]! A feature on your blog sounds amazing. I'm excited to hear what you think about it. Attaching the PDF to this email. Here are the review links in case you'd be open to cross-posting on Amazon[hyperlinked] or Goodreads[hyperlinked], No worries if not though! Just wanted to pass along the links in case you were."*

Strategy #7. Pay for NetGalley (and other resources)

Netgalley.com is a platform for reviewers to receive free books and write reviews for them. Many of the best publishers and distributors in the game are on it. This means that, while some of the deal sites can be inundated with unknown authors for readers, this one can have some of their absolute favorite all-time authors and publishers. If it's a benefit to readers, it's a benefit to authors.

But NetGalley is pricey and questionably worthwhile for indie authors footing the entire bill. If you've published only one book and don't have one on the horizon, you won't want to sign up for a solo account. But it's true that I've gotten customer reviews on pretty much every book I've put up on NetGalley. Not ten reviews, but not zero either.

Since it's a little pricy, I'd recommend checking out some NetGalley co-ops! This means that you and a bunch of indie authors split the cost so you don't have to pay a full membership fee for NetGalley, and you can have your book featured on there for a set amount of time. Xpresso Book Tours and Victory Editing are two sources for this, but more will pop up over time. You can even start your own!

You are probably not going to end up with twenty reviews from NetGalley alone, but it's a paid resource that puts your book to the test. Want to see how your book is doing with its current marketing—the cover, description, and eventual content. Reach readers by being on this platform.

Resources to make book review targeting easier:

1. **Bookfunnel or Storyorigin** — Automate the sending of your digital review copies with a sign-up link and review request reminders.

2. **Pubby.co** or **Pubnook.com** - Review other authors' books and then pitch those who are interested in yours.

3. **Book Award Pro** - Get editorial reviews and win awards.

4. (FREE) **Writer Watch**- Track when new reviews arrive online & protect from pirating.

5. (FREE) **PDF24** – Compress big files for sharing.

Strategy #8. Ask your following (newsletter and social media).

You should ask your followers to review your book. You shouldn't DM every single one of them or anything, but you should post about reviews on social media, schedule an email to go out requesting one, or put the review link in the footer of your emails.

Don't be too salesy in your social media post, and don't do it more than once—maybe twice. Sure everyone's not going to see it, but that's the nature of social media. I like using graphics to request reviews. It can be about reviews directly or simply about how to support you as an author, with reviews being near the top of the list.

You'll probably get more people to see your emails than your social media posts, so you'll want to ask there too. I like setting up a scheduled email—like thirty days after filling out a signup form—that requests a review with the review link. In addition to an automated email like that, you could also just send an email to all your subscribers on a day when you're set to email them. For example, I send emails every other Monday with Write Indie. I could ask for a review once in August or September for a book published in July.

The loophole here is using the same footer or signature in every email you send. The email doesn't have to be about your book or reviews at all. But if subscribers reach the bottom of the email, they could find your review link if you leave it there. You should have a link to buy the book for sure, but you could also add a link to a form where they can sign up to read it for free, leading them to a Bookfunnel or review team page.

Strategy #9. Hire a marketer or virtual assistant.

How do you make time for marketing your releases and writing your next book? It's not like you want to pawn off the fun stuff (writing), but good news is you can pawn off the time-consuming work of getting reviews.

Even if they don't have much experience in the publishing world, they could read this chapter and do all the things I'm telling them to do; hours of work, done.

But you can also get people with experience. It's just a matter of finding the right one; Reedsy.com is among my favorites for freelance marketers, or you can find cheaper virtual assistants on Fiverr.com, which will vary in quality.

Your assistant or marketer can write the pitches for you, or they can just put the list together while you pitch them personally. You may not find out how good their research ends up being until after you've pitched them, but you can guide them by telling them up front to exclude inactive reviewers and to avoid too many reviewer lists and directories.

Strategy #10. Sell direct on your website

There are benefits to enrolling in KDP Select. Placement in the Kindle Unlimited library, the free book promotions. I already talked about those. But there are benefits to making your books available elsewhere too. And plus, you can publish your paperback on all the other platforms even if your ebook is exclusive.

If you sell your book on your website, you can automate the review request process. This means that you don't have to ask for the review manually. Since they bought something from you and you're only sending one email related to the product, they don't have to choose to sign up with their email.

You can sell your book with a professional form on your website, like Forminator or FluentForms Pro. You just have to accept payments and edit the form settings so that when a person fills out the form (i.e. buys your ebook), they're added to a group in your email service provider. (I use Mailerlite.) Then you set up an automation sequence: people who join that group receive a confirmation email immediately and then fifteen to twenty days later, you thank them again for purchasing it and include the Amazon review link.

Strategy #11. Don't forget about Goodreads.

Goodreads ratings are starting to show up on Amazon pages. They have been for a few years now—even dating back to Amazon buying Goodreads in 2013—but it seems like Amazon is doing it more often now. And good news is—those Goodreads ratings are right there at the top of the product page, beside the Amazon ratings. Since some browsers only visit the top half of a product page anyway, it's smart to make time for Goodreads review targeting.

The Goodreads customer review guidelines aren't quite as strict as Amazon either. While Amazon will sometimes reject customer reviews if they violate conditions in their community guidelines or later remove them from your page, almost everybody (as long as you're not being abusive) can leave a review on Goodreads. It doesn't matter if they have the same last name as you, if you're Facebook friends, or if they didn't buy it through Goodreads links. If you want to get close friends to review your book, Goodreads is a good place to send them.

You can get more Goodreads reviews by finding reviewers on the platform through comp titles or you can try running Goodreads Giveaways. You have to pay for it—$119 as of September 2025—but you can give away up to 100 ebooks. The giveaway entrants have to be Goodreads users, so many of them are reviewing books already. And the best part: Goodreads emails the winners a few weeks after they've won to ask them to review it. An automated review request from a notable emailer—that's a BIG benefit.

I usually recommend going with the full 100 ebooks. You can choose to do 50 or 25 if you want, or you can do paperback giveaways. But if you're looking for more reviews, you'll want to shoot for the most readers possible.

Strategy #12. Mention it at your book event.

Sometimes a simple, in-person request can go a long way. No matter if you know the person who came to your reading or book signing or not, you can convince a reader to review your book even before they start reading it.

I like the soft, gentle angle of, "For those who grab a copy, let me know what you think in a review online, or even just an email!" Then, if they do email you, awesome! Thank them graciously and answer them personally, and if you want to share the review link in case they'd be willing to add it to Amazon, that could be a last-ditch effort to get that customer review up.

If it's a signing, consider pairing your book with a custom bookmark. It should be cool first and foremost, but then it could also feature a QR code or customized tinyurl link on the back of the design for the Amazon or Goodreads review page.

Sample Customer Review Pitch:

Subject: *Help your teacher cross over or be stuck in school forever? A gentle review request for* My Teacher Is a Ghost

Hi [Contact name],

I found your recent review of [Title] and loved what you had to say about it. I wrote a book that's pretty similar but also totally its own: It's about a magical middle schooler who needs to help his ghost teacher cross over, or he and his classmates will be stuck in school forever. Here's more about it [hyperlinked Goodreads link] if you want to take a look.

Could I send you a copy for review? It will be available on Amazon in March, but I can send the book over right now if you'd like it. I can reply with a digital copy (PDF or EPUB) or send a physical ARC. Just reply with your address, and I'll send it over.

-Tommy Tommerson

Follow-up – Seven days after first email

Just popping in for a quick follow-up! Would you like a free copy of my book? I'd love to hear what you think about it.

*And just for fun: since I contacted you last, it got a sweet review from Independent Book Review, calling it, "**A spellbinding work of middle grade paranormal horror that gives Stephen King a run for his money.**" Pretty cool!*

-Tommy Tommerson

Sample Customer Review Pitch (DM):

I love what you're doing for the Bookstagram community, [Contact Name]! Your book reflections are so personal and real. I love that. Do you take book requests? I just published a supernatural thriller with a badass ghost, kind of like [Title of recently reviewed book] but with a few twists up its sleeve. Want me to send it to you? Here's more about it [hyperlinked to landing page]. Would be happy to send you either a digital or physical copy for review.

16

CREATING LAUNCH AND STREET TEAMS

I want you to breathe during launch time. To celebrate. You're here. You made it. Give yourself time and space to feel proud.

Everybody's telling you to do a million things during launch week. You have to make a splash right away, they say. The Amazon algorithm likes that. You should have blurbs and customer reviews right away. You should have social media posts and newsletter mailings planned out for that week. Some extra publicity around then would be nice too. And that's not even mentioning in-person events—which you'll need books and a cake for.

Thing is: they're not wrong. All of those are good ideas. Launch time *is* important. That's why you want to start planning these things ahead of time, so you can party when launch day finally arrives.

You've already been pitching media before publication. It would be awesome if media or trade platforms timed their feature with your publication date, but I wouldn't depend on it. It's with the review gods now.

Instead, let's focus on what we can control: buyer excitement on social media and telling the Amazon algorithm and potential readers that the book is being read by real people in real time.

Let's build a launch team.

The concept is simple: gather fifteen+ of the most supportive people you know and ask them to be part of an organized effort to get reviews and social media engagement during one specific week. Let's get to it.

> # Design an online form for subscribers and followers to join your team.

Before you add supporters to your review targeting spreadsheet, let's see if anybody you don't know would like to be part of your team.

Create a simple Google form (docs.google.com/forms). Design a graphic as a header, share a short book description, and explain that they can read a free ebook before anybody else if they fill out this form and write a review for you. If you haven't yet, take a look at my form for this book for reference: TinyUrl.com/arcteamform.

After describing the task, you'll ask for the following responses:

- Name

- Email address

- On which platform they would leave their review

- Whether they would download a free copy of the book on Amazon before their review (available only for authors/publishers in KDP Select)

- Whether they'll help promote it on social media

You can share this form with your newsletter subscribers, your social media followers, and people who visit your website. If you don't have a following yet, this probably won't net you many reviewers, but those authors who have people looking at them already will likely add a few more names to their launch team. Just make sure to put the form in often-visited places, like your bio link on Instagram or your email signature.

Who to add to your launch team

Get out your review targeting spreadsheet. Crack your knuckles. Don't get up to pee or make coffee. Create a tab labeled "Launch Team," and in the first column, type the names of all the people you think would want to help you promote your book during launch week.

Include your best friends and your internet friends and your writer friends and your unpaid beta readers and your newsletter subscribers who filled out your form. You can write your mom or your significant other if you want, but I've got some caveats sneaking in here later about them.

I'll put a cap on this list at about twenty-five people. If you're not there yet, scroll through your social media followers to pick up anybody you might have forgotten about. It's totally okay to not get to twenty-five if you can't. I put a relatively high number here because I'm just trying to increase your review count as much as I can.

When I was putting launch teams together for authors, I was often met with a really good question: "Should I really be sending a book to people who I think would naturally just buy the book? Isn't that cutting into my sales?"

And the answer is yes! Some of the reviewers on your list will complete this task instead of buying your book in order to support you. Your biggest fans will probably do both, but it's true some of them won't.

And to that I say...include them anyway! Support looks different on everyone, and reviews can be even more valuable than a single purchase.

You should be working hard to increase actual purchases during launch week, but you can get those from strangers who won't review it. It's up to you in the end: If you feel like you'll only get one or the other and you want to hold out for a purchase, then that's totally fine.

Decide how you will contact them.

In column two of your review targeting spreadsheet, enter the email address or social media profile you'll be contacting.

I like email the most because you can CC your launch team all at once. But if your main relationship is on social media and that's where you think you have the best chance of turning them into a reviewer, then add the social media account you plan on direct messaging into their row. If you want to ask them first on social media DM for their email address, that could allow you to save some time in CCs later on.

When should you contact them?

The most important rule is to make sure your digital ARC is ready. It should be copy-edited and cleanly formatted, but unfinished formatting and proofreading errors are okay. You don't want to contact someone, have them say yes, and then tell them to wait. That's a reason you could lose them.

I like four to six weeks prior to publication to make your first ask, but you could talk me into eight. The trick is to not ask too far in advance because they can't leave reviews on Amazon until it's published anyway.

This amount of time also makes sure they have time to read it but not so much that they can forget about it.

Email #1. The first contact

I'm a big proponent of using the language "launch team" directly in your first message (no matter if it's on social media, email, or over text). People love to be part of a team. It creates a sense of comfort and community. You could just ask them if they'd be willing to help you out during launch week, but that's not quite as specific as telling them they are going to be part of an organized effort for you to get reviews and engagement during launch week.

Social media and text message work a little bit differently for a first contact. It can feel strange to put any promotional detail in a direct message to your friend. In these cases, it's best to pop in, break the ice with a line about the last thing you were involved in with them, and then ask them to join your launch team, without the praise.

Then, you'd tell them explicitly what would be expected of them if they agreed to join: read a digital book in around four weeks, engage with you on social media, and leave a review on Amazon a few days after publication. If you want to share a one-liner about what your book is about and why you think they might like it, that could be helpful to those who aren't sure if your genre will be right for them.

If they accept, you send them the book. You can either send the file directly through DMs or get their email. (Again, I'd recommend their email, so you can transfer point of contact over there.) While sending the PDF, thank them and let them know that you'll be in touch a few days before publication to remind them how to leave a review and support you.

Just a quick note to make sure your PDF isn't a two-page spread like you might get from Adobe InDesign; this PDF should be read one page at a time like readers would find it on a Kindle.

With email, you have a little extra room to personalize and professionalize your pitch. I like to start with the reason they are being contacted: "I was so glad to hear you liked my last book! Want to read my new one? I'm building a launch team..." Or, "How the heck are ya?" Something informal and personal could be a good way to break the ice and make sure they know it's not overly professional.

I recommend sending a batch of your pitches in the same day. You could do all of them if you have the time, but over a few days works too. Once you've sent the pitch, type the date in your review targeting spreadsheet. If they say yes, let them know how pumped and grateful you are and that you'll be in touch in four weeks.

Launch Team Pitch: Email #1 (Example)

Subject: *Will you be part of my launch team?*

Billy,

What is up!! It's been years. I keep wanting to reach out and ask a random question about your life, but I never know the right way to do that. So here it is: Did you quit on the Sixers yet?

I don't know if you've seen anything on social or anything lately, but I've got a book coming out in September! It's a weird little horror novella about a haunted school and a kid with a dimension-crossing walkie talkie.

Would you want to help me build some momentum by joining my launch team? I'm open to all kinds of help—like comments and likes and shares and whatnot on Instagram—but I'd be especially grateful for a review on Amazon during the first week of the book's launch. Would you be open to something like that?

I would send you a digital copy of my book, and you can read it over these next four weeks before the book comes out. Then I'd drop you a reminder and link for how to review it on Amazon.

Would that be something you're interested in? Totally okay if not or if this just isn't a good time for you. Just let me know!

Thanks! And even if it's a no, tell me what's been up with you and the kids! I'd love to hear from you.

-Tommy

How to follow up with prospective launch team members

Not everyone will answer the first time! And that is so okay. Emails aren't for everybody, and responding doesn't work out for a lot of different reasons for some people. Most of my conversion—whether blurbs, media, or customer reviews—comes from the follow-up. So don't feel bad about doing it.

Give your first contact a few days. I think five is a pretty ideal number, but six or seven works too. It's best not to be too quick or too long. Just drop by with something short and non-pushy, like this:

In reply to the original email:

> *Billy,*
> *Just checking in to see if you caught this! Would you join my launch team to help me promote my new book during launch week? Would love to have you on board!*
> *Tommy*

Email #2. A few days before publication

Five days before your release date, send your first email to your launch team. Blind Carbon Copy (BCC) everyone, not separate emails. This is where you'll do the bulk majority of your work in outlining what it is people can do for you.

What to include in email #2:

- Use a tone of excitement and appreciation.

- Thank them for offering to help.

- Remind them that they have a little over a week still left to finish reading.

- Share the specific date you expect the book to definitely be live on Amazon or other retailers. (Recommended: Wait about four days after expected pub date)

- Request that they engage with your social posts or make their own social posts on that day.

- Explain the next step: On the day of or after publication, you will email them again to share social media links they can engage with and share the review link. Tell them that they can review the book that day or be a superstar and wait seven days for the ebook to be free so they can download it first and then leave their review.

- Share even more appreciation and gratitude.

Launch Team Email #2 (Example)

Subject: *The countdown to publication is on! (A few more days before I explode.)*

Dear coolest launch team on the planet,

Thanks again for helping me launch my book! I love it and am proud of it, and I'm humbled by how many people want to help me bring it into the world.

My book is coming out in 5 days, August 4th! If you see me posting on social media that day or the days surrounding it, help me out with some engagement, will ya?! Likes, comments, shares, or your own posts—all awesome!

You don't have to do anything right now except for finish reading the book and keep an eye out for an email on August 4th or 5th.

On that day, I'll be dropping by with social media links and the review link. You can review the book right when you get it or you can wait seven days for my next email, where I'll ask you to download the ebook for free and then leave your review. By downloading, it will give your review a "Verified purchase" tag and help me become an Amazon bestseller in my genre.

For your review, you'll need to rate the book out of five stars, provide a heading for the review, and write a few sentences about it. It doesn't have to be 5 stars if you didn't love it, and it doesn't have to be long or poetic either. Just a couple lines about some of what happens in the book and what you liked or didn't like about it. You're not talking to me in the review but other readers.

Let me know if you've got any questions or concerns or anything. I'll be checking my emails feverishly over the next couple weeks, so I'll be more than ready to answer whenever you need it.

You rock. Thanks for being part of my team.

-Tommy

Email #3. The day of or after publication

Remember I told you to breathe?

Launch day is an important one for your mental health. I know how many things you feel like you have to do, and even how many things you want to do, but make the time to enjoy it too. Go outside. I hear it's nice out.

If you don't want to work on launch day, don't do it. Wait a day. But if you want your social media posts to do well and to read some (probably good) reviews right away, send your launch team email. BCC the whole group after your first social media posts go out.

Lead with excitement and honesty. Get them to understand, even just a little bit, how much it means to you that you have people behind you on this big day. But don't go overboard.

Aim to keep this email short. You're asking them to help you away from their inbox today, so don't add too much to their workload with an overly long email.

The most important things to hit are sharing the links to your social media posts and sharing the review link. If you are deciding on a free ebook promotion seven days after launch, you'll explain that too. And don't forget, if they reply to you, take the time to say thank you.

Launch Team Email #3

Subject: *My book came out today! Want to help me?*

My people,

My book has been published! It's real! I mean, look at this fancy page on the internet selling it: [Amazon/Bookshop shortlink].

Could you help me out today?

This is the link to post your book review: [Amazon review shortlink]. I'd love to hear what you think—but gentle reminder to not talk to me in the review but rather to other readers. If you want to download the ebook for free next week before leaving your review, then just wait for this step and move on to the next way to help.

My first social media posts just went out on all the platforms: [hyperlinks to specific posts]. Could you engage with them for me? Likes, shares, comments, your own posts—all great.

Thanks for being here with me today. It feels good to have somebody to talk to as I'm nervously refreshing Instagram.

-Tommy

Email #4. Four to seven days after publication

A few days after launch day, you'll pop in for another launch team email. If you're not doing a free download day, you'll want to wait the full seven days and send a follow-up email, since you already asked them to review the day of or after launch. If you are doing a free download day, you'll provide them with the book link to download as well as the review link. So let's do two samples:

For those who are NOT doing a free ebook promotion:

Subject: *Launch team - Thank you thank you thank you!*

Launch team,

Thanks for doing this with me! My book's been out a week now, and it's been a whirlwind of excitement and gratitude. I've gotten some reviews and people are telling me they're reading it, and it's all very heartwarming.

If you have already left your review, just know that it means a ton to me. If you see my book out and about on social media or strike up a conversation with somebody about books, I'd love it if you shared some love about it.

If you haven't left your review yet, it's not too late! Could you do it today? Here's the review link: [Amazon review shortlink]. Just a sentence or two would be huge.

And while this might be my last launch team email (sad face), don't take it as an excuse to disappear. Let me know if there's ever anything I can do for you or if you just want to say hi.

Until next time?

Tommy

For those who ARE doing a free promotion

> **Subject:** *Launch team - It's download and review day!*
> *Hey,*
> *Ready to help in a huge way?*
> *First, could you download the ebook on Amazon today? [Amazon ebook link]. It's free.*
> *After you download, could you leave your review here? [Amazon review link.]*
> *By downloading and then reviewing, you're giving yourself a "Verified Purchase" tag on Amazon and helping me hit the bestseller list.*
> *Appreciate you!*
> *-Tommy*

Street teams for books that are already out

A street team works a lot like a launch team. You ask people to be part of a team, and then you email that team three or four times during a set week to leave reviews and engage with you on social media.

If you want to do this, I'd recommend setting up some sort of promotion—like a free ebook for three days—and having the team download the book, review it, and then engage with it on social media during that week. Almost everything stays the same, except for some language about your book launching. Gather your team, tell them how to help, and leave the direct link before, during, and on the last day of the promotion.

If you can't do a free promotion—like if you're not choosing KDP select—you don't need to create a team. All you'd have to do is email them to review the book and, if they accept, send them a copy.

17

HOW TO USE CUSTOMER REVIEWS

C ustomer reviews communicate to potential buyers that your book is being read by everyday people, maybe like them.

You can absolutely use these types of book reviews—from reviewers with usernames like Tommy M. or CatLady402—to market your book, but using them is going to look different than the way you use blurbs and media reviews. You don't want to put **"This book rocks." - CatLady402** on your book cover, for example, even though I personally trust her with my life.

The #1 way to use these types of book reviews is...

To keep getting them.

You want your Amazon and Goodreads reviews to grow over time. Communicate to potential buyers that a lot of people read this book, and they keep reading it. If your review numbers keep growing, it tells readers that people are reading it *right now*. Not just right around publication time. This book could be relevant to them—could be a talking point with hypothetical bookish friends or not-that-bookish friends. These reviews work on their own as long as they're not predominantly bad. (Which you can probably salvage by getting more!)

But other than working all on their own, one of my favorite, under-the-radar ways to use your growing customer reviews to market your book is to screenshot them at milestones and share on your social media and newsletters. Let's talk about how to do that.

Social media

I usually recommend authors steer clear of posting about Amazon or Goodreads reviews on their social media accounts. Let your followers discover those reviews on their own when they visit the sales page. And plus—Amazon reviews are not blurbs from experts.

But you do have a few options, like:

- Screenshot your favorite customer reviews and crop them so they're just a small rectangle. Then design a graphic with a handful of the reviews pasted on there. The body of your post can be about how happy you are that people are enjoying your book. (Example on next page)

- If you have a lot of reviews, say over 50, I'd recommend screenshotting that number so that you can add it to an accomplishments graphic. This is particularly cool when you hit number milestones like over 50, 100, 200, etc.

- Post maybe one review that feels particularly heartwarming to you, like out of all the professional reviews you got, this real-person review means the most. This would be a personal post, so take your time talking about why it means a lot to you.

- Choosing a spotlight day of the week can help you post about multiple Amazon reviews, rather than just the one heartwarming one. If you make a theme out of it like, "Good News Mondays" or "New Review Fridays," your followers recognize that you're not just popping in willy-nilly whenever you get customer reviews and instead that it's something they can follow over time. This could work during the first few months after publication but not very long after that.

But know this! There's a fine line between organic social media use and looking like you're trying too hard. So post about customer reviews sparingly and be as genuine as possible.

Facebook Post (Example):

Gerri Almand: "I still can't believe how many people are out here reading and reviewing RV Wife four years after publication! Thank you to everyone who has read and left a review. Now get in the car and go."

(Source: *The Reluctant RV Wife* by Gerri Almand)

Newsletters

Just like with social media, you can definitely share a round of customer reviewer praise in your newsletter once. Maybe twice. The same components apply—post about review milestones, a particularly meaningful review, or a round-up of multiple.

Amazon A+ Content graphics

There's a fine line to walk here too! Some authors and publishers use a quote and attribute it to "Amazon reviewer," which I don't love. But if you haven't gotten any blurbs or have better material to use in the customer reviews section, you could design a full page of features on your Amazon page that highlights very short quotes from customer reviews instead of blurbs.

Here's how you could do that:

- Horizontal graphic at the top (like a banner) that says "What readers are saying about..." and then the title of the book in big font with a non-distracting, color-matched background on your front cover.

- Three square graphics with the very short quotes directly beneath that. I like one to three words best, but make sure they're great words. Avoid "Intriguing," "interesting," and relatable," and instead move toward "Pulse-pounding," "Breakneck pacing," and the "The best thriller you'll read this year!"

- Under there, you can do a horizontal module featuring something else: author bio, checklist, blurb from notable platform, hook-devoted graphic, etc.

The only way you should be using Amazon A+ content is if you're doing it well, so make sure you get feedback on any design you put up there.

Amazon lockscreen ads

If you're going to advertise on Amazon, you should be ready to experiment with a lot of different styles until they work. Sometimes you try a primary hook, a secondary hook, a blurb, and in another one, a single customer review quote. You can't attribute them by name, so you'll be forced to attribute it with "Amazon reviewer."

As you have probably guessed, I don't love it, but what matters is if it works. Some ads do better than others and you should have multiple ready. If it's a really good quote, go for it. And then, if it's not working after a good amount of testing, remove it.

Facebook ads

I like Facebook ads for those who have the budget to experiment—especially when running price promotions. You can only have a Facebook page (not a personal profile) in order to advertise, so if this is something you're interested in, create your Facebook page now.

Your ad should include some sort of graphic. You can put up the cover with a 99¢ symbol on it and nothing else, or you can add a review quote or multiple. I think graphics that highlight customer reviews should not use attribution and should probably be multiple short quotes. This requires some testing and experimentation too!

You can also screenshot the review and paste it in the middle of a color-popping background. Just don't do this if it's a negative review or something you're going to disagree with in the post.

Facebook Ad Example

Author: "Don't look under the desk. "

 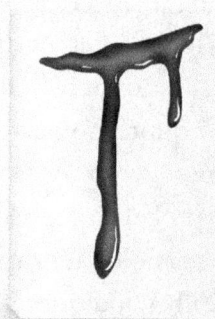

WHAT READERS ARE SAYING ABOUT TITLE

★★★★★

"Pulse-pounding!"

"Breakneck speed."

"A spellbinding work of middle grade horror that gives Stephen King a run for his money."

18

FINDING THE TRUTH IN CUSTOMER REVIEWS

C ustomers are everyday people. They find time to read where they can, and they know only what they know. They very well could be experts, but they also could be reading your genre for the very first time.

You can learn a lot about your author career through customer reviews, but it should be taken a little differently than reviews from professionals in your field or the book's field.

You get 0-2 customer reviews.

I find this scenario to be the least likely. Why? Because you're reading this book.

Implement the strategies I've recommended and actually take the time to carry them out. If you have pitched 100 reviewers and you've built a launch team and you still have 0 reviews, you should check your internet connection.

Don't be a book with no reviews on it. It's a sure-fire way to lose potential buyers the next time they find you.

You get 10 customer reviews.

This either means you tried a little bit or didn't try beyond the publication of the book. Don't stop. Keep searching reviewers on social media, keep finding new comp titles, keep sending one-off email pitches, and building review teams. This is a never-ending job. Don't end it.

If there's been criticism in each of those ten reviews, don't panic. Easy to say, I know, but these people are not experts who are unequivocally right. And sometimes they are straight up hurtful. You don't have anything to learn content-wise from your first ten reviews. Don't edit your book over it unless you have done something harmful and you can change it.

I think it's perfectly fine to read your reviews on customer review sites, but if you choose to stay away from them if they've been hurtful in the past, that's okay. Just keep an eye on that review count and keep pitching for more.

You have multiple 1-star reviews or ratings.

Don't panic! Depending on how many reviews you have overall, this probably means nothing. Three one-star reviews or rates but seventeen higher ones? Don't worry about it. Eight one-star reviews out of twenty? Now we're talking.

First of all, go get more reviews. Twenty is not enough of a sample size to tell you if you are doing things right or not.

But to get more reviews, you might have to take a second look at your genre, your description, and your cover. You could be getting reviews and purchases from people who are expecting something totally different than what you provided them. Make sure that's not happening. Rewrite your description if you notice those issues. Use different keywords or categories. These are pretty easy to do.

You can edit your book description via Amazon Author Central, even if you published with an indie press. Just make sure the formatting on the page looks clean when you're done; sometimes editing a KDP-uploaded description with Amazon Author Central can result in some wonky formatting.

The biggest impact move from a marketing standpoint would be to change your book cover. I'm not saying you should make that decision because a few people said they didn't like it in the customer reviews section, but I am saying that if you don't like your cover right now because it's admittedly bad, then you should do something about it.

After you improve your marketing, start review targeting again. Listen to how things are going. If you are still struggling to get them or gathering more one-star reviews, it could be the content of your book that is the problem. But I'd recommend asking an editor about that, not your reviewers.

You have a 4-star rating on Amazon with at least thirty-five reviews.

You're on the right track. This task takes time and effort and a salable book, so don't belittle it. But don't sit stagnant either. Hit fifty, I dare you.

I'd argue that 4 1/2 stars is better than 5 with that many reviews. They look real and genuine, and browsers are given the opportunity to explore varying opinions. It'll be up to them to decide whether the criticism sounds legitimate enough to stop them from buying or if they want to read it anyway.

Don't take the criticism too severely. One or two customers with a 3 or 4 star rating review doesn't make them an expert on the topic. But...eat up all the praise!

You get 50 book reviews on Amazon

I knew you could! 50 is a good number. You worked for these, and your book is making reviewers want to read it. There are so many other things to do in indie book marketing, so I grant you the gift of a break.

But hey, get back out there when you've got the stamina again. Add the reviewers you find on social media to your targeting spreadsheet. Keep engaging with previous reviewers. Stay active on your own platforms, and keep putting that "Leave a Review" link to work.

You get 100 book reviews on Amazon

Take a day off! Go somewhere nice. Have a party. Wear a crown for a day. Take this win and run with it. You are getting real feedback from real people, and you are giving your book the appearance of authority while pinging the Amazon algorithm.

Some people believe that getting a certain amount of reviews triggers Amazon to start pushing your book for you. But it's not public knowledge, and I'm not sure it ever will be. Hitting a number like 100 could be arbitrary, but you are using their platform the way they want you to. They have more incentive to reward you for it because books with more reviews sell better for them.

The short answer is that you have the answer. The truth. You are doing this thing right.

PART 5: THE INS AND OUTS OF REVIEW GRAPHICS

19

THE BEST WAY TO MARKET YOUR BOOK WITH GRAPHICS AND VIDEOS

I grew up in the 90s. I ventured through the early stages of the internet—those beautifully ugly webpages with large swaths of text, weird grey interfaces, autoplay music on homepages, and links on links on links to click. Now, it's become a visual cornucopia.

You might be a guerrilla in-person marketer, tossing hardcover books out your window to get sales from strangers, but if you want to get the most book sales, you're going to want to learn how to sell books online.

And one of the best ways to do that is by using images and videos to market.

The best way to drive engagement on social media

You don't have to do this. I repeat: you don't have to do this.

But if you want to—and you put in the time to do it well—you can thrive.

I'm talking about you. Using the real you. Pictures and videos of yourself will always do better on the internet than specially designed graphics and videos. People are following *you* on social media, not your book.

No matter if you're willing to do it all the time or just on special promotion days—like launch week especially!—if you put yourself in front of your followers, you'll achieve that ever-important level of marketing: the human one. It can be hard to think of people online as people in real life, but pictures and videos help break down the barrier.

Of course, those images and videos have to be well-produced. I'm not saying they've got to be fancy or you've got to be a model, but I am saying that you should be putting up unique, likable content if you're going to persuade people to support you.

I'd love to give you a big old list of content ideas for your social media or website, but we're still only focusing on book reviews here.

So here are a few of the ways you can use pictures or video of you to highlight your book reviews:

- In the caption of a photo of you.

- A reel: You in the shot with trending music and review quotes appearing on the screen around you.

- A reel: you discussing some nonfiction content in your niche.

- A reel: you narrating with a quote from within your book.

- A reel: you acting out a scene or trope in your book.

- You holding your paperback in a cool, relevant background.

- A book trailer with you in it or narrating it.

For the most part, when I'm talking about using real-you in social media, I'm talking about mentioning the review in the caption, not necessarily adding the words to the picture or video of you. The picture of you is the way in—the thing that catches their eye and makes them want to read more in the post's description. For example, "This is the look of a person who just got a starred review from Independent Book Review!"

> ## The second best way is when other people use their faces.

Other people posting themselves reading or talking about your book on their own platforms is extremely valuable. Whether you get them to do this as part of your launch or street team or you're pitching social media influencers to read and post about your book, you're doing a good thing by chasing after it. I'd put podcasts and YouTube interviews in this category as well; it's personal and real you and worth going for.

Seek out TikTok, Instagram, and YouTube influencers for these types of videos and posts.

20

How to Design Cool Review Graphics in 8 (Mostly Easy) Steps

Before I found Canva.com, I didn't believe in myself as a designer. I didn't have the eye, I thought. Didn't know what colors matched—ask my clothes!—which backgrounds to use, which fonts, how to make things even. Just trying sent me back to the time my first grade teacher told me if I couldn't color in the lines, I'd have to repeat it.

But...now I'm good at it?

Canva.com is a gift. Not only is it about as user-friendly of a design platform as you could ask for, it's legitimately fun to mess around with. Back when I was getting paid per hour to market for publishing companies, I kind-of-not-really-accidentally spent a lot of work time designing perfect, eye-catching graphics on Canva in the name of selling books.

And the thing was...it worked!

I posted those graphics on social media and newsletters, added them to our websites, to Amazon's A+ Content, and saw my time get rewarded with real book sales. Now it's your turn.

Step #1. Choose your graphic dimensions.

Instagram, Facebook, X, author websites, Amazon, email signatures—each place you plan to put a graphic requires its own size dimensions.

Some of these places require specific dimensions—like Instagram posts at 1080 x 1350 or header photos on X at 1500 x 500. Other platforms are more open-ended, like Facebook posts, but you'll want to design the right shape for your specific content. For example, I like vertical or square designs for quotes with a lot of words in them rather than horizontal designs. You have to make the decision eventually.

No graphic will do well if it's cut off by the platform's size requirements. If it doesn't tell you directly, just Google "Facebook cover photo dimensions for business page" and plug the numbers into Canva to get started.

For my example, I'm going to use a square design: 1080 x 1080. This works on Amazon A+ content and sidebars of most websites.

Step #2. Cut your longer review into a shorter quote.

Shortening reviews for graphics works a little differently than it does for shortening them in your Amazon editorial reviews section. For the most part, that means even shorter than usual.

For graphics, the amount of words/characters should be low. Twelve words is a bit on the longer side, but possible, while three to four words (as long as they're good, unique ones!) can work too. I usually find five to eight a nice sweet spot to give you room to design and enough language to make it laser-specific to your book.

Step #3. Add your front cover.

Did I already tell you how important your book cover is? Can I do it again?

It shows up everywhere! Especially in review graphics.

You can definitely create some graphics without your cover (like if you're going with brand colors and only an element of your cover instead), but most times, adding it is the easiest way to communicate which book the quote is talking about, who the author is, and what the vibe of the story is.

I like to add some shadow to book covers or use a 3D cover creator to make it look like a book and not just a picture.

Example (Steps 1, 2, and 3):

(for *Rewilding* by Lisa Gerlits; Illustrated by Savanna Durr; graphic design by Jordan McClendon-Spencer)

Step #4. Choose an attractive, matching background photo or element.

In Canva, you can scroll hundreds of pictures or elements that match your book's tone and vibe. I recommend typing in the colors of your cover or the ones that would accentuate your cover most.

I used to use background photos that matched the setting or theme of the book, but it does run the risk of overtaking the cover and quotes.

And those are the most important parts. So feel free to look for castles on Canva, but make sure it matches the castle in your book and doesn't take too much attention away from what's most important: that someone loved it. If you need to mute the background a little bit, you can blur it.

If you find a background that matches and looks good, choose it. Then maybe try to find a different one too. Don't worry yet if the photo seems a little too plain or if the text isn't fitting neatly in a gap in the photo. It would be great if those things happened naturally, but there are some solutions we'll get to soon.

Step #5. Choose the right font, font cover, and location of the quote.

This one's going to be obvious from the moment you choose a background photo: the font color is probably going to have to change.

Black (on light backgrounds) and white (on dark ones) are usually pretty dependable choices, but you can also match the colors included on your cover. You can either type in the color code you have from your cover designer, or you can see if Canva provided the cover colors directly in the editor.

Each design is different. I've been designing them for years, even when they use the same dimensions, and I still place review quotes in different places on graphics: Sometimes the cover is front and center, and the quote is on top or bottom; sometimes the cover is on the left, and the quote is on the right. Most important thing is that the cover is the first thing they see, and out of the periphery, that someone said something about it. The size of the quote also impacts where it's placed on the design.

And then enters my absolute least favorite part of designing these graphics: choosing the font!

There are hundreds of available fonts. I think I could spend my whole life finding the perfect one. It does matter though, so make sure you scroll and test with purpose. Maybe even duplicate your design a couple times so you can test out multiple fonts on the design you've already started. Sometimes the design is literary or academic, and so a simple, elegant font makes the most sense, while others are loud dark fantasy novels that require more of a mood. But while you're definitely shooting for the right mood, readability should remain your #1 priority. One of the easiest ways to choose fonts is to mimic the one on your cover.

Example (Steps 4-5):

Step #6. Use a background shape or text box to make the quote extra readable.

Sometimes you put the text in the right spot and you don't have to do anything else. Those are my favorite designs—when they fit into the background photo like it belongs there. It feels natural and eye-catching and requires no overcomplicating.

But sometimes the background photo doesn't have a neat empty spot where you can place text and still get the bulk of the photo in there. In that case, you can choose a shape or text box in the Elements tab to place behind the quote.

You will want to choose the right color—matching and/or blending it in is best, so you may have to edit or make more transparent to make that possible. I like squares, rectangles, rhombuses (rhombusi?), and purposely messier brush shapes.

Step #7. Add the quotation marks and attribution.

You can just use the quotation marks that are in the font you chose, or you can try a larger, more aesthetically pleasing mark straight out of the Elements tab in the Canva editor. No matter what you choose, definitely include the quotation marks. It's important for the viewer to recognize that you didn't write this compliment yourself.

Sometimes the shape you added behind the text needs lines to outline it so it doesn't look too pasted onto the picture. Lines—whether straight, dotted, thick, or thin—can help keep it professional.

And of course, don't forget to add who said the quote if you haven't yet: "-Independent Book Review" or "-Kirkus Reviews" or "-Steven Grier Williams, author of *Skadi and the Geats*." You may want the attribution to match the color of the quote or match the color of the quotation mark, background, or cover.

Step #8. Add an element relevant to the quote or book.

It might sound crazy because I just laid out seven other steps before this, but sometimes you do everything I've already told you and it still looks plain. Sometimes it needs a final "Element" to make it stand out and match. I am not talking about an additional photo to add on top of your design; just an element in the "Graphics" tab.

Maybe it's sparkles, maybe it's stars, maybe it's a cat or a moon or a silhouette of a spy with a gun for your noir thriller. In the sample below, it's flowers and a butterfly. All of it matters for your genre and quote. I like to make that element pretty transparent but still visible so it doesn't overtake the quote and cover too much.

Example (Final):

Alternative options to Canva

You can also use Bookbrush.com! I've enjoyed working with that platform, but the optionality and free elements available within Canva worked best for me. If you already have Adobe PhotoShop from your cover design, you can also use that. Not my personal favorite though!

If you do all this and feel like you're still not getting it right, no worries! Hire other people to do it for you. IBR can do it for you—ask a guy named Joe!—or you can find somebody on Fiverr.

21

THE (SHORT) TRUTH ABOUT USING VIDEOS FOR REVIEWS

You ever hear the phrase "Content is king," in marketing?

Well, let's switch that up a little for 2025. "Video content is king," especially in social media marketing.

With TikTok and Instagram reels breaking barriers for what we previously knew about going viral on social media, it's smart to adapt to the times and work your video magic. If you're going to use social media as a marketing tool, use it to its full capabilities.

You can post on your profile as much as you want on Instagram, but unless you're using reels and stories, you're not making as big of a splash as you can on that platform. TikTok is all video. It's got quite a complicated and rando-friendly algorithm too, so if you've got some video content in you, I say go for it.

But as you already know, this is going to be a short chapter. Not because videos aren't awesome and useful, but because the best way to get good video content on these platforms is to be reviewed by popular accounts or for you to do something completely unrelated to book reviews.

You can definitely get creative and use review quotes to spice up your video presence, but your videos will be more successful when you're being funny, dancing, and doing other things unrelated to promoting your book. Get popular as an account first, turn them into fans, and then sell your book organically.

Here are some ways you can still use reviews in your video content:

- Use an animation to make the text of a review type out. Use shifting background photos and an element like a slip of paper where the text is appearing. Don't use the whole review. Just a snippet.

- Put a review in the caption of your video and talk about how it made you feel.

- Use popular music.

- Narrate a page from your book with a cool video background and then add a review quote and cover on the final slide.

- Design a book trailer that uses short snippets of reviews like movie trailers do.

Overly promotional material can have mixed, if not ineffective results on social media. People know when you're pushing when all they want to do is scroll. But when it's done well, naturally, and actually fun—you can make it work.

PART 6: SECRET TIPS AND RESOURCES

22

WRITE BOOK REVIEWS TO GET MORE BOOK REVIEWS

Welcome to my absolute favorite way to get more book reviews.

And it's not because you're destined to get tons of book reviews from it. You will get some, but that's not why.

It's because it helps everybody.

Make some time in the months leading up to your book's launch and through your book's publication to review fellow indie authors' books.

It's against Amazon's policy to customer review swap overtly—meaning, I scratch your back, you scratch mine—but you can definitely review other authors' books to help you get them yourself.

In this chapter, we'll talk about writing blurbs, publishing reviews on literary websites, and more.

Write blurbs for other authors in your niche.

You're an author now. (Or are soon to be one). You have something to promote. And putting your name and book title on someone else's cover can increase your name recognition.

If a fellow author asks you to blurb a book for them, say yes. You can also offer the idea to them, but the blurb market is usually the authors/presses asking for who they want, not accepting the people who ask them. You can definitely float the idea by an author if you want, but I wouldn't spend time targeting books to blurb. If they weren't thinking of you before, they're probably not putting your name on their cover. Maybe on their Amazon page though, if it's a good one!

If you haven't written a blurb before, it can feel like strange new territory. You're not writing a big old book review because it won't fit on their book covers. You'll be asked to write about three sentences to encapsulate what makes the book special, and then the author or publisher could use an even smaller quote from those sentences in their marketing.

One of my favorite formulas for blurbs is this:

- A super short and enticing first line of praise

- A super short summary of what happens that's unique to this book

- A recommendation at the end related to the audience: "If you like Lauren Groff and Dantiel W. Moniz, you'll love this moody Florida novel about real people doing real things."

If you've published with an indie press, email the marketing department and ask if they have anybody you can blurb. Most presses love to get blurbs from their authors. Everybody helps everybody in that situation.

Publish reviews in media and trade outlets.

Some trade platforms are looking for reviewers! If you've got time and like to read free ebooks, go back to the media review section in your spreadsheet and visit the platforms' websites. This time, you'll look for if they are hiring freelance book reviewers.

In many cases, these outlets pay. Many of them don't pay enough for it to be a full-time job, but it can be a fun side-hustle where you use the money to fund your writing career. If you leave all the money you make reviewing books off to the side to use for your own book marketing, you can have plenty down the road to pay for stuff you wouldn't have paid for previously.

Even if you don't get a freelance job doing it, you can still publish well-written reviews in media outlets. I've made so many online friends by writing reviews for them. It's among the best gestures you can do for an indie author. You already know how hard they're working to get them. Get on their good side by doing it without them even asking. They'll remember it. And maybe, in the future, they'll want to promote your book on their own social media or help you out with a blurb or review.

Join a community of authors.

If you join a community like Pubby or Pubnook, you sign up to review other authors' books. You cannot review swap with them directly—meaning I review your book, you review mine—but you can find other reviewers to pitch on the platform. You pay a small fee per month, but the communities are active and the reviews are real.

The more you connect with other authors, the more you'll find support. That's yet another benefit to doing things like joining local writers' groups, writing organizations, attending conferences and readings, becoming a beta reader, and promoting other people's books on social media. Nobody knows how important reviews are like other authors. Don't be pushy of course. Connect genuinely with these people, and perhaps the next time you have a book coming out, they'll sign up to be on your launch team.

23

HOW TO GET GOOD REVIEWS

G ood books have a better chance of getting good reviews than worse ones. That part's obvious. Quality always comes first. Hire editors, get beta reader feedback, transcend expectations, enthrall. Write the best book.

But you can also influence good reviews simply from the marketing and presentation of your book. So let's do it.

Send it to the right person.

There's no better way to get good reviews than to target reviewers accurately. At Independent Book Review, I ask my reviewers to state their genre preferences directly, and then I have them update their genres as much as they want. I always want to stay on top of their growing interests. The chances they write a good review for a book they wanted to read are higher than one they were simply assigned to review.

I learn much more about my reviewers when I read what they're saying in their book reviews. I'm not saying you have to read every review from every reviewer, but I am saying the more you learn about them and what they love, the more you can cater your pitch and future projects toward them. And you'll get more good reviews when you do.

Sure you may get reviews if you send emails to every contact you find on the internet, but your reviews are going to be worse if you're targeting the wrong readers. I don't send pitches to reviewers outside of their genre interests; people who don't read much fantasy usually won't offer the same nuanced praise as someone who reads it regularly. Seek out that nuance.

Be respectful and modest in your pitch.

Relationships are of the utmost importance in book review targeting. Build them early and often. If you seem like a good, genuine person at the time of your pitch, reviewers will be more inclined to support you with a good review.

The best way to do that is to personalize your pitch (at least a little) and avoid giving yourself or your book too many compliments. You can let other people do that with review excerpts pretty harmlessly though!

Make it clear from the beginning that you're not expecting anything from them. Pushiness and asking for specific timelines when they'll be finished are ways to give the reading experience a sour taste.

Provide what you promised in the description.

One of my favorite things to do with book descriptions is pepper keywords in there. I'm not totally convinced it helps the search-ability of your book on Amazon, but it helps the Amazon AI reader and offers little pulse-points for the right kinds of readers.

But if you're going to mention it in your description, it should play a real part in your book. For example, if you mention a friends-to-lovers storyline to influence a sale or review, it should be fulfilled in the book. Don't let it be secondary characters and romances we aren't asked to invest in. When you do follow through on that promise, readers feel like they got what they came for.

This is especially true of nonfiction books. If you promise in the Introduction of your self-help book that you're going to give practical steps to losing weight by improving nutrition, this book should come with actual step-by-step instructions and timelines.

Send your book in a fun package.

One sneaky marketing way to get good reviews is to make it incredible from the moment a reviewer receives the book. This is why I like including little freebies in physical ARCs for reviewers. Stickers are cool and bookmarks are too, but you can go outside of the box too: I've seen people design original art for their street teams and (once) even send a snake-eraser wrapping around a pencil for a book with a snake character.

You make reviewers so excited to open a box that they open it on their Instagram Live, and you're upping the chance that they enjoy the reading experience. I wouldn't call it bribery exactly, but I would whisper it. This also connects with digital files. If they request a specific kind of file, take the time to get it for them.

Use an Advance Praise page.

This tip is one of my favorites, but it only works if your blurbs are good.

If a blurber mentions that you do something spectacularly well and a new reviewer doesn't know exactly what they loved about your book, they can read the blurbs to get started on their review. It makes it easier on them, and it doubles down on the amount of reviewers talking positively about your book.

When you put blurbs in an "Advance Praise" page at the beginning of your book, you allow reviewers to work directly from their ereaders. They're more accessible that way and a good reminder for reviewers to consult them.

Provide a summary sheet of previous books.

Is your book part of a series? Help a reader out! Not many of us jump at the prospect of reading later books in a series if they're not standalone stories, so you may want to share a summary sheet of what they need to know from previous books.

Buy another review.

If you bought an editorial review from a review company, you're getting a review from one specific reviewer. But all reviewers don't read the same. Everyone's tastes are different.

So if you got a paid review that came in a little lukewarm, you can ask the company if they'd be open to you buying another review. Many companies—like mine—have no problem sending your book to another reviewer for another perspective. This is obviously about as optional as it comes since everyone's budget is so specific to them, but it doesn't hurt to know.

24

WHAT TO DO WITH BAD REVIEWS

Bad reviews happen. If you get enough reviews, you're bound to get some negative ones mixed in there. It's just math. Show me the book that's gotten over 100 reviews and all of them are five stars, and I'll show you my skeptical face.

It can feel pretty brutal to get a review with negative criticism. That's why so many authors stay away from their Goodreads pages. Sometimes they're not helpful, not open-minded, and can get mean. And despite getting ninety-five good reviews, the other five could be the ones you just keep thinking about the next time you sit down to write book two in your series.

I'd love to give you permission to ignore them, but I think I'd rather talk you through what to do when you receive them.

Don't respond to them.

I know it can be tempting. You visit Goodreads and see that the most recent review is one star and gets details wrong about your book and misunderstands the point of it. This happens.

But you're not going to talk them out of it. And if you do respond, other readers can see it. The best thing for you to do when you receive a bad review is to read it and move on.

If you pitched this book to that reviewer and they let you know over email that they completed their review, answer them for sure, but just to say thank you. Don't defend yourself, ask an extra question, or ask them to take it down (unless they offer). Sometimes bad review ratings can actually help how the book appears on these rating sites. 4 or 4 1/2 star averages look a whole lot more genuine than hundreds of 5 star reviews.

Should you accept the publication of your review?

Sometimes a review company or reviewer shares an unpublished review with you prior to posting it because they want your permission beforehand. If that review is a negative or mixed review, you may be tempted to tell them not to publish the review.

And in some cases, sure. You can definitely turn them down if they say your book is harmful, offensive, or not worth buying.

But I almost always recommend saying yes. Someone writing about your book is a good thing, and while strangers and prospective buyers could find that bad thing they said about your book, many of them will either skim the review—and maybe miss the negative—or treat it for what it is: someone's opinion. They might even disagree with that person before reading and have it inspire them to buy the book just to see if the reviewer is right. Reviews are for readers first and foremost, and giving them more content to engage with is a good thing.

Should you use quotes from a mixed or bad review?

Yes! You can definitely still use positive quotes from a mixed review. Many reviewers include positive takeaways from books they didn't absolutely love. And if you're looking for blurbs from those reviewers, you can still use them.

If you place a pull-quote from a mixed review on your Amazon editorial reviews section, they're probably not going to Google the rest of the review. I wouldn't recommend including any criticisms in that editorial reviews section, but the good stuff can definitely stay.

Can you get the review taken down by Amazon?

If you think your review is misleading or abusive, you can report it to Amazon to have them take it down. You can either hit "Report abuse" underneath the negative review or contact community-help@amazon.com. Once you describe why you felt the review was unfair, their team will investigate and decide (without telling you the result) whether or not it will be removed.

I wouldn't waste your time with this unless they left the review by mistake, like if it was for the wrong product. I've also seen some reviews get removed if the product was published by KDP and it came with printing errors, like the wrong book inside of it. If it's just a negative review of your book—even if it's just short and kind of mean—they're probably not going to remove it.

What if you've gotten bad reviews but fixed the problem?

They still won't remove that review. You can edit the book and re-upload, but the review won't go away. The only way it would is if you unpublished the book and republished it with a different ISBN. But you'd also lose all of your other reviews if you do that.

Should you listen to bad book reviews?

I've seen a lot of advice over the years about the importance of ignoring bad reviews. I don't know if I agree with that all the way.

Criticism is a part of this. Writing is art. People like it or they don't, and sometimes they tell you why.

But that doesn't mean they're right either. It's just what they felt—and it's true to them—not necessarily to every fellow reader they're talking to. But the only way to get better at this thing called writing is if you absorb it, let other reviewers chime in, and count how many times that problem has been mentioned. If ten readers all said the same thing and you only have fifteen reviews, they might be right.

Can I ask reviewers to edit their reviews?

For content, no. Definitely don't ask them to fix their opinions based on additional detail, but you can ask them to edit their reviews if they contain glaring typos or incorrect factual information, like calling the main character Lola when her name is actually Leyla. Most publications would be totally okay to make fixes like this, but for Amazon reviews, don't worry about it at all. These are real readers; they're not supposed to be perfect or correct 100% of the time.

Should you edit your book after getting reviews?

There are so many benefits to self-publishing. The money's one of them, and the creative control is neck and neck with it.

If you decide you want to make changes to the book based on review feedback, you can edit the book without having to republish. If you published with Ingram Spark, you may have to pay a fee to do it, but with KDP, it's free.

But you shouldn't do it all the time, and you should really, really believe in that change. Maybe even loop your editor in on the idea. Offensive material is among my top tier list of things worth editing, but I'm also on board if you want to substantially improve the book on a structural level because you plan on continuing to promote it.

25

HANDLING BOOK REVIEWS AS A SMALL PRESS AUTHOR

Small presses rule. Some of my all-time favorite books come from publishing houses that are made up of four people in random basements, spending their precious time trying to get people to read books they love and those they think provide value.

I also love small presses from the author's side. Sure you don't have the same royalty rate and you don't have full creative control, but having a professional team behind you can make way for more reviews, especially from trade publications. This could be because of connections, clout, experience, distributors, and a quality barrier. Self-publishing is amazing, but the traditional publishing model makes way for at least a little gatekeeping. Someone else believes your book is ready to sell.

But publishing with a small press does come with some caveats too, the main one being that the publisher might not believe in a certain marketing strategy.

What publishers usually have the final say on:

- Adding graphics to your Amazon page (A+ Content)

- Printing physical ARCs before publication

- Sending books for review on their own dime

- Price

- Discounted or free promotions

- Blurbs on your front or back cover

- The review request at the end of the book

- Giving you a PDF or EPUB for fear of pirating

What to do if they don't want to do something you want to do.

Say okay.

Going with an indie press is more than just getting help with publishing your book. It's also about trusting their vision and allowing them to do their job.

You can definitely ask for every single one of the above tasks. Most publishers want your book to sell too, so if you show them that you're trying to sell it for them in strategic ways, they could be open to changing their policy for you. But as always, do it with respect and understanding. These people are working for free to sell your book, and you want to stay in their good graces.

The one thing I'd ask twice about is getting a workable, e-reader-friendly PDF. Some presses have been ripped off in the past—their book was taken by a fake reviewer and ended up selling a lot of copies despite donning an eye-patch and peg-leg. In your request, reassure them that you'll take good care of it and vet the reviewers as much as you can before sending them a copy. It's true that some platforms and reviewers only accept PDFs, so you should try to get that. EPUBS are good to have too though, since you're trying to make it as accessible as possible for your reviewers.

What you can do without your publisher

- Add blurbs to your Amazon editorial reviews section

- Change your book description through Amazon Author Central (but check the formatting afterwards!)

- Advertise on Amazon and Facebook

- Send copies to reviewers

- Research which of the publishers' previous books were reviewed on which platforms and pitch that platform while highlighting the indie press's name and previous book.

- Reach out to fellow authors from the press to see if they'll blurb your book or help you promote it on social media. Just make sure to offer to do the same for them.

Think like an indie press.

When you have a lot of books to promote, you can't promote all of them. Or at least all of them equally. And you wouldn't want to.

Some books sell better than others. Publishers have the receipts to show for it. When another book enters their queue with high-selling points, they may consider it a lead title and put more time and money into it than a different, less-splashy title. If you get chosen as one of these books, rejoice. If your book doesn't fit that mold or the press has less time than they envisioned at the time of your publication, that's okay too. You're still going to be doing the same amount of work in marketing whether your book is a lead title or not.

Conclusion (Or How to Do This Whole Thing Right)

I made a promise to you.

If you actively target book reviews, you will be able to tell if you are doing things right.

You have my knowledge now. The results of my experiences. You recognize what it takes to convince a reviewer to say yes, and you know which outlets to contact, how to contact them, and how to follow up respectfully.

But you won't know the truth until you get out there yourself.

Don't get discouraged. Don't panic if it turns out you've done a few things wrong along the way. All you can do is use these constantly developing truths to help you pave the way for a smarter, more effective author career.

It's a shame the timeline starts with blurbs and media reviews. Anyone who's been out there pitching knows—it's an extremely humbling thing to reach out to giants (or, at least, taller people) in the industry. I put the word "humbling" in most of my blurb requests for a reason. You're shooting for the stars right away, and the system is designed for most of them to either say no or not reply altogether.

If you leave these processes feeling dejected, don't panic and think that your truth is that your cover is bad, your description is bad, your book is bad and needs to be burned. You could be hearing crickets for reasons out of your control—some blurbers don't write blurbs these days because they can't expend the time anymore, or trade reviews aren't taking bites on you because they received 200 other book pitches today, and yours doesn't come with a big name or notable publisher.

Keep pitching, keep improving your pitch, and keep your head up.

As long as you put in the work, you'll find out your real truth in the form of genuine, varied book reviews. You'll find out what your audience wants, and you'll satisfy them.

And that's what we're in this for. To write a thing real people respond to.

I have been whispering as I type this book, and it would make me feel a lot better if I knew that someone other than the people looking weird at me at Panera right now were listening. It doesn't matter if you have to ask people to read your book. It's not something to be ashamed of; it's something that can make your whole career worth it.

Find your readers. Learn from them. And then your readers will find you.

Before I release you to the book marketing wolves, I put a to-do list in the back of this book. There are a lot of things to do, so I wanted to outline some of the most impactful for you: pre-publication, pitching, launch, and beyond. As long as you do your damndest, you're giving yourself the best chance to figure out if you are doing this whole thing right.

See ya in my inbox.

- Joe

THE TO-DO LIST

BOOK REVIEW MARKETING IN 40 STEPS

THE TO-DO LIST

BOOK REVIEW MARKETING IN 40 STEPS

PHASE ONE: BEFORE PUBLICATION

1. ☑ Write a great book.

2. ☐ Design an amazing cover.

3. ☐ Write a damn good book description.

4. ☐ Design a good website or landing page.

5. ☐ Take a professional author photo.

6. ☐ Get ISBN.

7. ☐ Add book & author profile to Goodreads

8. ☐ Create a dynamic QR code and Redirection link leading to your Goodreads book page.

9. ☐ Add a review request to the end of your book, using the dynamic QR code and redirection link.

10. ☐ Sign up for email marketing service. (Mailerlite, Mailchimp, etc.)

THE TO-DO LIST

BOOK REVIEW MARKETING IN 40 STEPS

PHASE TWO: PITCHING

11. ☐ Get review targeting spreadsheet at IndependentBookReview.com/WriteIndie.

12. ☐ List matching categories, keywords, & comp titles in spreadsheet.

13. ☐ Find & list media outlets in spreadsheet.

14. ☐ List potential blurbers in spreadsheet.

15. ☐ Pitch blurbers (3-9 months pre-pub).

16. ☐ Pitch trade reviewers (starting at six months pre-pub).

17. ☐ Design blurb graphics for announcements & Amazon A+ Content.

18. ☐ Pitch & follow-up with media outlets 3-4 months pre-pub until 1 year post-pub.

19. ☐ Pitch customer reviews two months pre-pub until forever.

20. ☐ Add reviews to website/landing page.

THE TO-DO LIST

BOOK REVIEW MARKETING IN 40 STEPS

21. ☐ Build launch team (2 months pre-pub).

22. ☐ Plan & schedule social media launch week announcments (1 month pre-pub).

23. ☐ Create ARC team signup form and add to website and newsletter.

24. ☐ **Publish your book. Celebrate. Breathe.**

25. ☐ Switch Dynamic QR code link from Goodreads to Amazon review page.

26. ☐ Switch Redirection link from Goodreads to Amazon review page.

27. ☐ Create Amazon Author Central Account.

28. ☐ Add blurbs & graphics to Amazon.

29. ☐ Engage with commenters and supporters on social media launch posts.

30. ☐ Email launch team with review link 1-7 days post-pub.

THE TO-DO LIST

BOOK REVIEW MARKETING IN 40 STEPS

PHASE FOUR: AFTER PUBLICATION

31. ☐ Automate an email one month after subscribing to ask for a review.

32. ☐ Post about incoming reviews on social media.

33. ☐ Write blurbs for other authors.

34. ☐ Update the signature in your email & newsletter with a review signup link.

35. ☐ Update your editorial reviews & graphics when better blurbs arrive.

36. ☐ Stay active, engage with others, and find new reviewers on social media.

37. ☐ Run periodic eBook promotions.

38. ☐ Review fellow authors' books at Pubby.co or an alternative.

39. ☐ Advertise on Amazon & Facebook.

40. ☐ Write more books.

HELP ME BREAK THE BOOK
REVIEW SOUND BARRIER

This is a book about book reviews. If anybody knows how much they mean to authors, it's you. And if I'm going to help authors, I could use your help doing it.

Will you write a review for me? Good, bad, medium, whatever—as long as you mean it, I'll be grateful. For this niche book marketing book, I'm setting the sound barrier at 100—can you get me there?

Tell me what you think in a review by typing **IndependentBookRe view.com/ReviewLink** into your search bar, scanning the barcode below, or sending me an email at jwalters@independentbookreview.com.

ACKNOWLEDGMENTS

This book wouldn't exist if it weren't for my people.

Thank you to Isaac Reyes for asking me what my dream job would be. To Jeremy Solomon for taking a chance on me at Inkwater Press; to Vanessa, Andrew, Holly, Masha, and Sean, who helped me feel at home there. To Morgan Gist MacDonald of Paper Raven Books for asking me about my wins and taking me behind the scenes of customer reviews. To Lawrence Knorr of Sunbury Press for publishing so many books, for listening to my ideas, and for his patience when my world changed because of tiny humans.

To my editors and beta readers over the years, including for this book, like Jaylynn, Alex, Gary, Kate, Rankin, Randal, Emily, Tucker, and the others at Literary Arts in Portland and Grub Street in Boston.

To all the books and the writers who have shaped my knowledge and craft over the years, like Ray Bradbury, Joanna Penn, Matthew Salesses, Joe Biel, Laura Stanfill, Matt Bell, David Gaughran, Dale L. Roberts, Rob Eagar, Penny C. Sansevieri, Courtney Maum, and so many more. And of course, to all of my writers at IBR and all the authors and publishers who've supported us and believed in us since 2018.

Thank you to my dad, who was the first writer I knew, and my mom for the forever-support and the gentle nudges to finish my work. To my in-laws for so much, but especially the breakfasts, the office, and the way you love my little people.

And most of mosts—thank you, Jaylynn. I couldn't have done this—any of it—without you.

About the Author

Joe Walters is the founder of Independent Book Review. He has been the marketing director for Inkwater Press, a book review and metadata specialist for Paper Raven Books, and a marketer for Sunbury Press. In his Write Indie newsletter, he shares writing motivation and industry tips with indie authors who are looking to find more readers. When he's not writing, assigning, or editing reviews in a Pennsylvania Panera Bread, he's playing with his daughters or reading indie books by Kindle light. Check out which ones at IndependentBookReview.com.